Explosive Business Growth Strategies

GANE Ontario

Ira Bowman & Joel Phillips

Chuck Coxhead, Carol Putnam, PhD, Dr. Andrea Renee Rivera, Eric Rosen, Fritz Colinet, Rick Loek, Amy Lau, Sheila Jones, Brad Smith, Shelby Jo Long

ISBN: 979-8-89079-045-3 (hardback)
ISBN: 979-8-89079-044-6 (paperback)
ISBN: 979-8-89079-046-0 (ebook)

CONTENTS

DIGITAL MARKETING SHOULD CENTER AROUND YOUR WEBSITE'S SEO

IRA BOWMAN

Digital Marketing in today's business world should begin with a website. Search engine optimization (SEO) should be a priority, as it is the key to getting Google to help rank your website higher. By improving your rankings on Google, you can help ensure that you always have a steady stream of prospects in your sales pipeline. There are five pillars to ensuring your website is primed for Google and that, if implemented correctly, can help you increase your SERP (search engine results page), aka where you rank on Google compared to your competition.

This chapter will review all five pillars of your website, including structure, content, speed, backlinks, and visitor traffic.

SECTION ONE: WEBSITE STRUCTURE

- **Metadata:** Metadata is the data that provides information about other data. In the context of websites, metadata is the information that tells search engines what your website is about and how to index it. This includes the title tag, meta description, and image alt text.

- **Alt descriptions:** Alt descriptions are the text that appears when an image cannot be displayed. Search engines also use them to understand the content of images.

- **H-tags:** H-tags are HTML tags used to structure a web page's content. They are used to create headings and subheadings, which help search engines understand the content hierarchy on your pages.

- **Schema:** Schema is a markup language used to add information to web pages. This information can be used by search engines to better understand the content of your pages and to display richer snippets in search results.

- **Site map:** A site map is a file that lists all the pages on your website. Search engines use it to crawl and index your website more effectively.

- **Robot.txt file:** A robot.txt file is a file that tells search engines which pages on your website they should crawl and index. This can be used to prevent search engines from crawling certain pages, such as password-protected pages or pages containing sensitive information.

- **Broken links:** Broken links point to pages that no longer exist. They can damage your SEO because they can give search engines the impression that your website is not well-maintained.

- **Error pages:** Error pages are displayed when something goes wrong, such as when a page cannot be found or when there is a problem with the website's code. Error pages can also damage your SEO because they can give search engines the impression that your website is unreliable.

All these factors can affect the structure of a website and, in turn, its SEO. By following best practices for each of these areas, you can improve the structure of your website and boost your SEO rankings.

Here are some additional tips for improving the structure of your website for SEO:

- Use clear and concise navigation menus.
- Organize your content into logical categories.
- Use internal links to connect related pages.
- Make sure your pages are well-optimized for keywords.
- Keep your website up-to-date and free of errors.

By following these tips, you can create a well-structured and easy-to-navigate website, which will help you improve your SEO rankings.

SECTION TWO: WEBSITE CONTENT

Of the five pillars, most people think they have this one nailed down solid; however, when I review websites day in and day out at Bowman Digital Media, I find most are missing the mark with website content, too. What's mainly missing is the written content in volumes that can help satisfy Google when your website is indexed (content cataloged by Google for use later when people search a topic) monthly.

Keep these key strategy tips in mind for your website content moving forward.

- **Written content:** The amount of written content on your website is essential for SEO. Search engines like Google want to see that your website has a lot of high-quality content so they can better understand your website and rank it accordingly.

- **Video content:** Video content is also becoming increasingly important for SEO. Search engines are starting to index video content, which can be a great way to attract visitors to your website.

- **Interactive media:** Interactive media, such as images, audio files, and slide decks, can also be a great way to improve your website's SEO. These types of media can help break up your text and make your website more visually appealing, leading to more visitors and higher rankings.

Here are some additional tips for creating compelling website content for SEO:

- **Optimize your content for keywords:** When you're writing your content, optimize it for keywords you want your website to rank for. This means using those keywords throughout your content, titles, meta descriptions, and headers and sub-headers.

- **Make your content informative and engaging:** Your content should be informative and engaging so that visitors will want to read and share it with others. This will help to improve your website's traffic and rankings.

- **Keep your content fresh:** Keep your content fresh by updating it regularly. This will show search engines that your website is active and that you provide valuable content to visitors.

By following these tips, you can create website content that is effective for SEO. This will help you to attract more visitors to your website and improve your rankings in search results.

Here are some additional thoughts on the specific points mentioned above:

- **The amount of written content:** I recommend you include at least 1,500 words on each page that you want to rank on Google. This is a good starting point, but it's not a hard and fast rule. The amount of content you need will vary depending on your page's topic and the competition you're facing. However, in general, more content is better than less regarding SEO.

- **Video content:** Video content is a great way to break up your text and make your website more visually appealing. It can also help attract visitors to your website and keep them engaged. If you're able to create high-quality video content, it can be an asset for your SEO efforts.

- **Interactive media:** Interactive media can also be a great way to improve your website's SEO. These types of media can help break up your text and make your website more visually appealing, leading to more visitors and higher rankings.

SECTION THREE: WEBSITE SPEED

How important is website speed for SEO?

Website speed is a significant factor for SEO. Google has stated that page speed is a ranking factor, and studies have shown that faster websites rank higher in search results. There are a few reasons why website speed is essential for SEO:

- **User experience:** A slow website will provide a poor user experience, which can lead to users bouncing (leaving without any interaction) from your website. This can negatively impact your SEO rankings, as Google considers bounce rate a ranking factor.
- **Conversions:** A slow website can also lead to lower conversion rates. If users wait too long for your website to load, they may be less likely to complete a desired action, such as purchasing or signing up for your email list.
- **Indexing:** Google's crawlers need to be able to access and index your website quickly. If your website is slow, it may take longer for Google to index your pages, which can delay your rankings.

WHAT IS AN IDEAL TIME FOR THE PAGE TO LOAD TO SATISFY GOOGLE?

Google has not officially stated the ideal time for a page to load. However, they have said they aim to load most pages in under two seconds. In 2021, Google announced it would use Core Web Vitals as a ranking factor. Core Web Vitals is a set of metrics that measure the loading experience of a web page. One of the Core Web Vitals metrics is First Contentful Paint (FCP), which measures how long it takes for the first piece of content to render on a page. The ideal FCP for a page is 2.5 seconds or less.

HOW TO IMPROVE WEBSITE SPEED

There are several things you can do to improve the speed of your website:

- **Optimize images:** Images are often one of the most significant contributors to website slowness. You can optimize your images by reducing their file size and using a content delivery network (CDN).

- **Minify and combine CSS and JavaScript:** Minifying and combining CSS and JavaScript files can help reduce the size of these files, improving loading times.

- **Use a caching plugin:** A caching plugin can help store static files on your server, improving loading times for subsequent visitors.

- **Move your website to a faster host:** If it is hosted on a slow server, you may consider moving it to a faster host.

By following these tips, you can improve the speed of your website and boost your SEO rankings.

SECTION FOUR: BACKLINKS, BOTH INTERNAL AND EXTERNAL

Backlinks are links (clickable word/s) from one website to another. They are also known as inbound, incoming, or one-way links. Backlinks are essential for SEO because they signal to search engines that other websites find your content valuable. The more backlinks you have, the more authoritative your website will appear to search engines, which can lead to higher rankings in search results.

Backlinks work because they are a way for search engines to understand the relationship between websites. When a website links to your website, it is essentially saying that it is a valuable information source. This helps search engines understand that your website is relevant to the topic of the linking website, which can lead to higher rankings in search results for those keywords.

An internal backlink is a link from one page on your website to another page on your website. They are also known as intra-links or self-links. Internal backlinks are important for SEO because they help search engines understand your website's structure and the relationships between your pages.

There are two types of backlinks: internal and external.

First, let's look at internal backlinks. Internal backlinks work because they are a way for search engines to understand the importance of different pages on your website. When a page has a lot of internal backlinks, it signals to search engines that the page is valuable. This can help the page rank higher in search results.

There are a few different ways to create internal backlinks, including:

- **Using your navigation menu:** Your navigation menu is a great place to create internal backlinks. When you link to other pages on your website in your navigation menu, you are telling search engines that those pages are important.
- **Using your footer:** You can link to the most important pages in your footer, such as your Homepage, About page, and Contact page.
- **Using your content:** You can also create internal backlinks in your content. When you reference another page on your website in your content, include a link to that page.

By creating internal backlinks, you can help search engines understand your website's structure and the relationships between your pages. This can help your website rank higher in search results.

Second, external backlinks point to any place on your website, known in SEO terms as "off-page." External backlinks, or inbound links or backlinks, are links from other websites to your website. They are one of the most critical factors for search engine optimization (SEO). External backlinks signal to search engines that other websites find your content valuable. The more backlinks you have, the more authoritative your website will appear to search engines, which can lead to higher rankings in search results.

Here is some additional information about external backlinks:

- **Dofollow backlinks:** Dofollow backlinks are the most common type of backlink. They pass on link juice, which measures the authority of the linking website.
- **Nofollow backlinks:** Nofollow backlinks do not pass on link juice. They are often used for social media links or links to irrelevant websites.
- **UGC backlinks:** These backlinks are created by users, such as in comments or forum posts. They are often considered more valuable than website backlinks, as they are a sign that real people find your content valuable.

External backlinks work because they are a way for search engines to understand the relationship between websites. When a website links to your website, it is essentially saying that it is a valuable information source. This helps search engines understand that your website is relevant to the topic of the linking website, which can lead to higher rankings in search results for those keywords.

There are a few different ways to get external backlinks, including:

- **Create high-quality content:** This is the most important thing you can do to get external backlinks.

If your content is valuable, other websites will naturally link to it.

- **Guest blogging:** This is a great way to get backlinks from high-quality websites. When you guest blog, you write a blog post for another website and include a backlink to your website in the author bio.

- **Social media:** Sharing your content on social media can help you to get backlinks from other websites. When you share your content on social media, include a link to your website.

- **Commenting on blogs:** Commenting on blogs is a great way to get backlinks from other websites. When you comment on a blog, include a link to your website in your comment.

By following these tips, you can get external backlinks to your website and improve your SEO rankings.

SECTION FIVE: VISITOR TRAFFIC

Visitor traffic is significant. The other four things discussed in this chapter help create more visitor traffic by getting Google to promote your website higher in the SERP, as discussed in the chapter opening. Visitor traffic, repeat visitors, and new visitors are essential for SEO.

- **Visitor traffic:** Visitor traffic is the number of people who visit your website. It is a measure of the popularity of your website and can be an indicator of your website's SEO health.

- **Repeat visitors:** Repeat visitors visit your website more than once. They are valuable to your website because they are more likely to convert into customers or leads.

- **New visitors:** New visitors visit your website for the first time. They are a potential source of new customers or leads, so making a good first impression is important.

All three types of visitors can help improve your SEO rankings. Visitor traffic shows search engines that your website is popular and that people are interested in what you offer. Repeat visitors show search engines that your website provides value to its visitors, and new visitors can help you reach a wider audience.

Here are some tips for increasing visitor traffic, repeat visitors, and new visitors to your website:

- **Create high-quality content:** This is the most important thing you can do to increase visitor traffic. If your content is valuable, people will be more likely to visit and return to your website.
- **Optimize your website for search engines:** This means using keywords throughout your content and ensuring your website is easy to navigate.
- **Promote your website on social media:** This is a great way to get new visitors.
- **Run advertising campaigns:** This can help you to reach a wider audience and attract new visitors to your website.

By following these tips, you can increase visitor traffic, repeat visitors, and new visitors to your website, which can help improve your SEO rankings and grow your website's traffic and audience.

SEO SUMMARY TO GENERATE MORE SALES VIA DIGITAL MARKETING

Here is a summary of how site structure, content, speed, backlinks, and visitor traffic can all help boost SEO:

- **Site structure:** A well-structured website is easy for users and search engines to navigate. This means using clear and concise navigation menus, organizing your content into logical categories, and using internal links to connect related pages.

- **Content:** High-quality content relevant to your target keywords is essential for SEO success. This content should be well-written, informative, and engaging. It should also be optimized for keywords throughout the text, title tag, and meta description.

- **Speed:** A fast-loading website is user-friendly, and user-friendly websites tend to rank higher in search results. This means optimizing your website for speed by reducing the size of your images, minifying your CSS and JavaScript files, and using a caching plugin.

- **Backlinks:** Backlinks are links from other websites to your website. They signal to search engines that other websites find your content valuable. The more backlinks you have, the more authoritative your website will appear to search engines, which can lead to higher rankings in search results.

- **Visitor traffic:** Visitor traffic shows search engines that your website is popular and that people are interested in what you offer. This can help your website to rank higher in search results.

Following these tips can improve your website's SEO and boost your rankings in search results.

Digital marketing has a lot of components with social media, ads, emails, newsletters, guest posting, and more. If you are trying to drive traffic, don't forget that the lion's share of visitors are using Google, so your strategy should be heavily concentrated on SEO for your website. If you implement the lessons taught in this chapter, your website should perform well, and you will likely have no problem attracting prospects for your sales team so they can work with warm leads and consistently fill the sales pipeline.

About the Author

Professionally, Ira Bowman is a marketing and sales expert, photographer, graphic designer, website builder, philanthropy owner, Search Engine Optimization content writer, published author, and TEDx speaker.

Ira holds a bachelor of science degree from Liberty University, where he graduated with a 3.916 GPA in interdisciplinary studies, with a concentration in business and religion. This says a lot about who Ira is, as he has many interests and strives to do things with excellence.

Over his 25-year career, Ira has worked in the restaurant, e-commerce, print, and marketing industries. Most of Ira's career has been spent in a sales role in the print and graphics industry, helping small and medium-sized businesses gain market share and increase sales. Since June 2020, with the launch of Ira's business, Bowman Digital Media, Ira has focused on helping increase visibility for his clients on social media and increasing website traffic. The internet has become the primary source of commerce, and visibility is essential to increase sales.

THE HIDDEN DIGITAL TRANSFORMATION: HOW TECHNOLOGY IS RESHAPING BUSINESS AND CUSTOMER INTERACTIONS

JOEL PHILLIPS

INTRODUCTION

In the twenty-first century, digital transformation has evolved from a technological buzzword to a business imperative. According to a study by IDC, an overwhelming 85 percent of enterprise decision-makers believe they have two years to make significant inroads into digital transformation. Failure to do so could result in financial setbacks and a loss of competitive edge.

This chapter aims to comprehensively analyze how digital transformation is revolutionizing how businesses interact with their customers. It will also delve into the seismic digital marketing shifts and the challenges of the evolving advertising landscape. Then, we will explore the future and where the subsequent paradigm starts. Finally, we will see what it has in store for how business is done today and how that transforms into how business will be done tomorrow.

The Evolution of Digital Marketing

A Decade Ago

Ten years ago, the digital marketing landscape was in its infancy. Businesses were primarily focused on achieving as much online visibility as possible. The metrics used to measure the success of digital campaigns were relatively simple and often limited to the number of clicks or impressions. Social media was still nascent, with platforms like Facebook and Twitter just starting to gain traction among businesses as tools for customer engagement. However, these platforms were not as sophisticated as today regarding analytics and targeting capabilities. The primary focus was quantity over quality; going viral was the goal of any digital marketing campaign.

Five Years Ago

Fast-forward to just five years ago, and the landscape has already seen significant changes. The advent of advanced analytics tools and customer relationship management (CRM) software allowed businesses to delve deeper into customer behavior and preferences. According to a report by IDG, 44 percent of companies had moved to a digital-first approach by this time.

This shift meant that businesses were focusing more on the quality of the interactions rather than just the quantity. Email marketing has become more sophisticated, with companies using data analytics to segment their customer base and deliver more personalized messages. The era of "spray and pray" marketing ended, replaced by more targeted and data-driven strategies.

A Year Ago

The most recent changes in the digital marketing landscape have been driven by the rapid advancements in artificial intelligence (AI) and the Internet of Things (IoT). According to statistics from Statista, an estimated 15.14 billion connected devices will be online by 2023.

This proliferation of connected devices has given businesses unprecedented access to consumer data, enabling them to develop highly personalized and targeted marketing strategies. AI algorithms can now analyze this data to accurately predict consumer behavior, allowing businesses to fine-tune their marketing strategies in real-time. Chatbots have become a familiar and necessary feature on websites, providing instant customer service and gathering valuable data simultaneously. These tools are still exceedingly underutilized.

The Decline of Traditional Advertising

Noise in the Marketplace

Traditional advertising channels like TV, billboards, and print media are becoming increasingly ineffective. One of the primary reasons for this decline is the sheer volume of information and advertisements that consumers are bombarded with daily.

According to a study by the American Marketing Association, the average consumer is exposed to up to 10,000 brand messages daily. This sensory overload has led to "ad fatigue," where consumers become desensitized to advertising messages, making it nearly impossible for brands to stand out. Most advertisers and marketers try to increase the volume to help their clients get found, but this is proving ineffective, much to the frustration of marketing budgets in almost every industry. The rise of ad-blockers and filters designed to reduce the noise has further complicated the landscape, with users now having the tools to actively avoid advertisements.

DATA PRIVACY AND THIRD-PARTY COOKIES

In the name of privacy, companies like Apple and Google are heralded for restricting third-party access to marketing data. However, we must look closer before lauding these privacy efforts. They aren't protecting the consumer as they would have you believe. Simply put, they are protecting their data by putting a fence around it where the only people who can access it are themselves.

Most people only have half the story when Facebook lost, in one day, over $232 billion in market capitalization. They don't know that the Apple marketing platform picked up most of that market cap since they can still reach and retarget their own consumers.

Retargeting is the reserving of the same ad on a different platform. When you see an ad on Facebook and then see it elsewhere, it is because you were retargeted via cookie or pixel. This type of ad made advertising cost-effective, but little did everyone know that cutting off third-party access to data would eliminate or severely hamper ROAS (return on ad spend). Apple owns 40 percent of the market, and Google owns 60 percent. One guess as to who, in 2023, is restricting third-party access to data.

Moreover, the discontinuation of third-party cookies and pixels due to data privacy regulations like GDPR and CCPA has severely impacted the ability of businesses to track user behavior and preferences. According to eMarketer, 30 percent of internet users are expected to use ad blockers by the end of 2021, adding another layer of complexity to the already challenging advertising landscape. This has led to a significant shift in how businesses approach data collection and analysis, emphasizing first-party data and more transparent data collection methods. However, most businesses are still blind to this.

THE RISE OF COMMUNITY AND ONLINE INTERACTIVITY

BUILDING COMMUNITIES

Many businesses are turning to community-building and online interactivity to cut through the noise and connect with their target audience. According to Accenture, 75 percent of consumers are likelier to buy from a brand that recognizes them by name, knows their purchase history, and can make personalized recommendations.

Online communities provide a platform for businesses to engage with their customers more meaningfully, offering value beyond the transactional nature of traditional customer-business relationships. Still in its infancy, companies are now investing in building strong online communities around their brands, providing a space for customers to interact, share experiences, and even contribute to product development.

The Importance of Interactivity

As a starting point, interactive content like quizzes, polls, and highly engaging videos are becoming increasingly popular as they offer an entertaining way for customers to engage with brands. These interactive elements increase user engagement and provide businesses with valuable data on customer preferences and behavior. Gamification, the application of game-design elements in non-game contexts, is also one of the many tools used to enhance customer engagement and loyalty.

The Future of Digital Marketing and Customer Interaction

As we look to the future, it's clear that digital transformation will continue to evolve and shape how businesses interact with their customers. According to Gartner, 56 percent of CEOs have reported that digital improvements have led to increases in revenue. This suggests that businesses investing in digital transformation will likely see a significant return on investment, but how do you keep up? Advanced technologies like AI, machine learning, and IoT will play a pivotal role in shaping customer experiences, offering personalized, real-time solutions that meet individual needs and preferences.

Summary

The digital transformation is a tectonic shift redefining the fabric of business operations and customer interactions. According to Smart Insights, with 34 percent of companies having already started their digital transformation journey, it's evident that this is more than just a trend; it's the future of business. Companies that fail to adapt risk becoming obsolete as technology continues to plow forward and redefine the rules of engagement in the digital age.

The statistics and trends make it abundantly clear that it will be far more costly if you don't act now, and could even put you out of business. Businesses must embrace these changes and invest in digital transformation strategies to remain competitive in this ever-evolving landscape.

THE NEXT STEP: THE CONVERGENCE OF AI, AR, DATA, AND BLOCKCHAIN

A NEW BUSINESS MODEL

The future of business is not just about adopting a single technology but the convergence of several disruptive technologies. Artificial intelligence (AI), augmented reality (AR), data analytics, and blockchain are revolutionizing industries. However, when these technologies converge, they promise to create a new business paradigm, redefining how companies interact with clients, prospects, and their operational models. This convergence is not a mere speculation; it's a reality unfolding before our eyes. Businesses that fail to adapt to this new paradigm risk becoming obsolete. The stakes are high, and the time to act is yesterday. Technology doesn't wait for us to figure it out, but it does demand that it be appropriately applied.

The Convergence Explained

Artificial Intelligence (AI)

AI is already making waves in customer service, data analysis, and decision-making processes. Advanced machine learning algorithms can predict market trends, customer preferences, and potential supply chain disruptions. The future will see AI integrated into nearly every facet of business, from automated customer interactions to real-time analytics that provide actionable insights. The AI algorithms of the future will be self-learning, capable of adapting to new data without human intervention. This will make them incredibly efficient at solving complex problems that would take humans much longer.

Several questions continue to plague altruistic naysayers regarding the use of AI in the business world, and we need to take a quick detour to visit these questions before moving on.

Q: Should society question the use of AI in business?

A: Too late. AI is already too ingrained, and there is no turning back now, so we may as well embrace it and use it responsibly.

Q: AI is bad for business and will replace much of the human workforce.

A: The same thing was said about computers, and the adoption of computers created more jobs. Same with AI. Mainstream, commercial AI has been around since around the time that Amazon started their projection engine back in the '90s, where they made product recommendations based on the items you were purchasing. The adjustment period started a long time ago and is accelerating.

Q: The potential for AI to be dangerous is severe, and we need to consider this before adopting AI into mainstream business.

A: This is probably the most critical point:

1. First, most people don't know that Merriam-Webster changed their definition of AI from having reasoning capabilities to handling automated tasks. AI does not reason nor take action that it is not programmed to take.

2. Second, it is agnostic to good and evil. If it takes a bad action, that is because it was instructed to take a bad action, and just like with any hacking scenario, if you put up a wall to prevent a bad action, nine times out of ten, someone will find a way around it. It is dangerous because it is so powerful.

3. Ninety-nine percent of the danger in AI is contained in its ability to mimic. Initially, AI could mimic four human behaviors four to five levels deep. Then, it evolved to playing chess and mimicking intricate and complex models. Now, it can mimic millions of levels deep in an instant, making responses, deepfake videos, deepfake audio, images, and more impossible to discern between real and fake. Guess what? Here comes a derivative of NFT. (That is for another book.)

AI in Customer Service

Imagine a world where your customer service is not just automated but personalized. AI can analyze customer behavior, purchase history, and even social media activity to provide a service that is both efficient and personal. This level of personalization can significantly increase customer satisfaction and loyalty, giving businesses a competitive edge.

Augmented Reality (AR)

AR is not just for gaming; it's an enormously powerful business tool, and we have barely scratched the surface. Whether virtual try-ons in a retail store or complex data visualization in a board meeting, AR enhances user experience by blending digital information in the real world. In the future, AR could be used for real-time simulations, employee training, and much more.

There are so many unrealized applications for AR, and we are just getting started. Some forward-thinking companies have already begun testing augmented reality in the marketplace.

AR in Retail

Imagine being at home or walking into a store where you can see how furniture would look in your home before even buying it. Or a clothing store where you can try on clothes virtually. This is not science fiction; it's already here, and it's being made possible by AR.

Data Analytics

Data is the lifeblood of modern business. Companies generate massive amounts of data, but the analytics turn this data into actionable insights. Advanced data analytics can deeply understand market trends, customer behavior, and operational efficiencies. Data analytics will be the backbone for decision-making in a converged technological landscape.

The Power of Real-Time Analytics

The future is not just about collecting data; it's about collecting data in real-time. Real-time analytics can provide businesses with insights as events happen, allowing them to make more informed decisions faster. This can be particularly useful in industries like finance, where market conditions can change in the blink of an eye.

BLOCKCHAIN

Blockchain is far more than just the technology behind cryptocurrencies. Its potential for creating secure, transparent transactions is nearly limitless. It is also a means for unchangeable data validation. In a business context, blockchain could be used for secure contracts, transparent supply chain management, and even for establishing verifiable trust between parties.

Blockchain in Supply Chain

Imagine a supply chain that is not just transparent but also immutable. A blockchain-based supply chain would allow businesses to verify the authenticity of products from manufacture to delivery. This could be particularly useful in industries like pharmaceuticals, where the authenticity of products is crucial.

THE IMAGINARY MODEL: BUSINESS IN THE NEXT FIVE YEARS

Imagine a world where a customer enters a retail store, and facial recognition technology identifies them as they enter. An AI-driven customer service bot greets them by name and offers personalized shopping suggestions based on real-time data analytics. As they move through the store, AR-enabled displays allow them to interact with products in a way that has never been possible. A blockchain-based system ensures a secure, transparent transaction when they decide to purchase.

But it doesn't stop there. In the future, businesses will operate on decentralized networks, with AI algorithms making real-time decisions based on a constant data stream. Thanks to blockchain, supply chains will be transparent and verifiable, and customer interactions will be more personalized than ever, thanks to the insights provided by advanced data analytics.

In this model, the convergence of these technologies creates a seamless, efficient, and highly personalized customer experience. Businesses that adopt this model will see increased customer engagement and significant cost savings due to these technologies' automation and efficiency.

The Impact on Business and Society

The convergence of these technologies will create a ripple effect beyond just business operations. It will redefine employment, requiring a workforce skilled in new technologies. It will also raise ethical and security concerns that must be addressed at a societal level. According to data from Proshark, companies that are early adopters of these converging technologies are already seeing a 25 percent increase in operational efficiency and a 35 percent increase in customer engagement.

Challenges and Ethical Considerations

While the potential benefits are enormous, there are also significant challenges and ethical considerations. Data privacy, job displacement due to automation, and the ethical implications of AI are just a few of the issues that need to be addressed. Regulatory bodies and ethical frameworks will be crucial in shaping this new landscape.

Summary

The convergence of AI, AR, data analytics, and blockchain is not just a possibility; it's a certainty. The businesses that will thrive in this new landscape will be those that can adapt and integrate these technologies into their operational and customer engagement strategies. The future is a converged technological landscape, and it's closer than we think.

THE FINAL PIECE: THE PARADIGM SHIFT IN BUSINESS OPERATIONS AND CLIENT RELATIONS

WHAT DOES THIS MEAN FOR HOW WE DO BUSINESS TODAY?

The previous sections have laid the groundwork for understanding the seismic shifts occurring in the business landscape. Section 1 focused on the current challenges in digital marketing and client interactions, emphasizing the noise in the marketplace and the limitations imposed by the discontinuation of tracking as we know it using tools such as third-party cookies and pixels.

Section 2 took us into the future, exploring the convergence of AI, AR, data analytics, and blockchain as the new business paradigm. This final section aims to tie these two narratives together, illustrating the significance of these impending changes and offering a roadmap for businesses to navigate this complex landscape.

THE SIGNIFICANCE OF IMPENDING CHANGES

The convergence of disruptive technologies like AI, AR, data analytics, and blockchain is not just a futuristic concept; it's a reality already taking shape. Companies that stay in touch with what is happening around them are beginning to realize that the old ways of doing business are becoming obsolete.

Traditional advertising methods are losing their effectiveness, and the ability to reach clients through digital means is becoming increasingly challenging. According to data from Proshark, businesses that have started to adopt these technologies are seeing increased customer engagement and operational efficiency.

Here is where the danger lies. Those organizations capable of monitoring external events and understanding the importance of keeping up, especially in the speed-of-light state of technology we are in, will survive and thrive. These are typically mid-tier or more prominent companies with dedicated technology and marketing teams performing constant and consistent research to at least remain status quo.

What about everyone else? All those companies starting out or in the growth curve stage that prevents them from dedicating time and resources to the expensive effort of staying competitive in the marketplace, what do they do to maintain or get ahead? This population is the majority, not the minority, and the answer is simple, but it's not.

The short version is that technology companies will have to change to develop a conduit for most businesses worldwide and deliver the solutions that are already becoming necessary for small to medium companies to survive, much less thrive.

THE URGENCY OF ADAPTATION

The need for adaptation is not a matter of if but when. The digital landscape is evolving at an unprecedented rate, and businesses that fail to adapt will be left behind. The urgency is further compounded by global economic uncertainties, making it imperative for businesses to be agile and responsive to market changes.

The Immediate Impact on Today's Business

The changes are not just for the future; they affect business today. Companies not adapting to these changes find competing in the marketplace difficult. The noise level in digital advertising has reached a point where it's increasingly challenging to capture the attention of potential clients. Businesses must start adopting new technologies and strategies to reduce this noise.

The Cost of Inaction

The cost of inaction will be severe. Businesses that fail to adapt to the new technological landscape risk losing market share, customer loyalty, competitive edge, and customers. According to Proshark, companies that have been slow to adapt to digital transformation have already seen a 20 percent decline in customer retention rates.

Changes Needed for Survival

Businesses need to make several fundamental changes to survive and thrive in this new landscape:

1. **Adopt New Technologies:** Companies must invest in AI, AR, data analytics, and blockchain to stay competitive.
2. **Personalization:** With the decline of third-party cookies, businesses need to find new ways to personalize customer experiences. AI and data analytics will help fill this gap.
3. **Transparency and Security:** With increasing concerns about data privacy and security, adopting technologies

like blockchain provides transparency and security that customers are beginning to demand.

4. **Community Building:** In a digital world filled with noise, building a community around your brand can provide a level of engagement that traditional advertising methods can't achieve. But be forewarned: Building a community is more than just collecting names, a little data, and sending regular messages. It is about building a relationship with each consumer, which means understanding them without violating their privacy. That is a tricky balance.

THE NECESSITY OF STRATEGIC PARTNERSHIPS

In addition to adopting new technologies, businesses should consider forming strategic partnerships. These partnerships can provide access to resources and expertise that may be beyond the reach of an individual company. For example, a small retailer could partner with a data analytics firm to gain insights into customer behavior, or a healthcare provider could collaborate with a blockchain startup to improve the security of patient records.

THE PARADIGM SHIFT'S IMPACT ON DIGITAL FOOTPRINT AND CLIENT RELATIONS

This paradigm shift will significantly impact a company's digital footprint. The convergence of these technologies will allow for a more personalized, secure, and engaging online experience, which in turn will positively impact digital marketing strategies and client relations. Businesses can target their audience more effectively, provide personalized services, and build stronger client relationships. Your website must know your visitors and clients without being invasive.

The Evolution of Customer Expectations

As these technologies become more integrated into our daily lives, customer expectations are also evolving. Customers now expect more personalized, convenient, and secure interactions with businesses. This expectation shift requires businesses to rethink their approach to customer engagement, moving away from transactional interactions to building long-term relationships.

Projected Timelines

Minimum Projected Timeline

- **1–2 Years:** Early adoption phase where businesses integrate AI and data analytics for personalized marketing.
- **3–5 Years:** Widespread adoption of AR for enhanced customer experiences and blockchain for secure, transparent transactions.

Maximum Projected Timeline

- **5–7 Years:** Near-complete convergence of AI, AR, data analytics, and blockchain, leading to a new business paradigm.
- **8–10 Years:** The new business paradigm becomes the standard, and companies that have failed to adapt risk becoming obsolete.

The Variables Affecting These Timelines

It's important to note that these timelines are not set in stone. Various factors, such as economic conditions, regulatory changes, and technological advancements, could either accelerate or delay these projections. Therefore, businesses must remain flexible and prepared to adjust their strategies as needed.

CONCLUSION

In the grand tapestry of business evolution, we have explored the interconnected threads that weave a compelling narrative of change, challenge, and opportunity. First, we laid the foundation by examining the current state of digital marketing and client interactions, highlighting reduced effectiveness caused by market noise and the adoption of ever-increasing privacy challenges that directly impact the ability to track behavior online. Then, we catapulted into a future shaped by the convergence of AI, AR, data analytics, and blockchain, offering a glimpse into what a business will look like. Finally, we tied all these elements together, emphasizing the urgent need for businesses to adapt and evolve.

BRIDGING THE GAP FOR SMALL AND MEDIUM BUSINESSES

One of the most significant challenges small and medium businesses (SMBs) face is the lack of resources to compete with giant corporations with in-house technology and marketing departments.

These larger companies have the competitive advantage of leveraging cutting-edge technologies to optimize their operations and customer engagement. Rapid advancements in technology have created tools capable of leveling the playing field. Still, the companies must be able to implement these technologies, and that ability is historically beyond the budgets of SMBs.

Technology companies will have to alter their business model to serve a different type of market. Forward-thinking outfits specializing in technology solutions, like <u>Proshark</u>, see the value in raising the tide and are making it easier for SMBs to access the same level of technological sophistication that was once the exclusive domain of larger corporations.

The Role of Fractional Technology Departments

Stepping in to act as fractional technology departments for SMBs, future-focused companies, like Proshark, understand the increasing need for the technology function in every company. Fractional makes it affordable.

These partnerships go beyond merely providing a service or a product; they offer a comprehensive suite of solutions tailored to the unique needs of each business. From implementing AI-driven customer relationship management systems to integrating blockchain for secure and transparent transactions, these technology companies enable SMBs to survive and thrive in this new landscape.

The Multifaceted Role of Tech Companies

The role of technology companies in this new paradigm is multifaceted. They serve as consultants, implementers, and long-term partners. They assist with tech functions ranging from data analytics and customer engagement strategies to cybersecurity measures and blockchain implementations. By doing so, they empower SMBs to focus on their core competencies, secure in the knowledge that experts in the field are handling their technological needs.

The Future is Collaborative

The future of business is not a zero-sum game where only the largest corporations survive. It's a collaborative ecosystem where businesses of all sizes can leverage technology to offer value to their customers. Companies like Proshark are at the forefront of this shift, offering a lifeline to SMBs in a sea of technological complexity.

Final Thoughts

The convergence of the challenges and opportunities outlined in all three sections presents a compelling case for immediate action. The paradigm shift is already underway, and its impact on digital marketing, client relations, and the competitive landscape will be profound.

The time to act is now, and the roadmap has been laid out. Businesses, regardless of their size, need to adapt to survive in this rapidly evolving landscape. The future belongs to those prepared to adapt, evolve, and collaborate. Future-focused technology companies are not just service providers but strategic partners in this journey toward a new business paradigm.

By understanding and integrating the insights from this chapter, businesses can better prepare for the seismic shifts reshaping the industry. The future is not a distant horizon but a dynamic landscape shaped by our daily decisions. And in the future, collaboration, innovation, and adaptability will be the currencies of success.

About the Author

A seasoned entrepreneur, Joel is CEO and founder of Proshark and founder, CTO, and global managing partner of the Strategic Advisor Board. He has extensive experience in leadership, innovation, software development, automation, app development, data sciences, analytics, cybersecurity, and real estate.

He serves on multiple boards and believes the next step in technological evolution brings the convergence of blockchain, artificial intelligence, augmented reality, and data sciences.

- Member of Mensa, Bellwether, and ACA
- Licensed real estate broker with commercial development experience
- Resume includes 4G Development, Sony Pictures Digital Entertainment, eAssist Global Solutions, and American Loans
- Volunteer work includes J Ryley Foundation, Habitat for Humanity, and Planning Commission Chairman
- Hobbies include flying, sailing, golfing, biking, music, and music production

Be an Anomaly

Chuck Coxhead

Cure Your W.I.N. Disease

A crucial part of selling requires that you shed your personal needs. I know I'm asking a lot. W.I.N. disease is an affliction that is born from self-preservation. It is an instinctual survival behavior. For some of us, it manifests as a highly competitive nature. For others, it may be vanity. In most, we have developed a habit of thinking about ourselves and what we need to accomplish in a given day—which is a lot.

We or I Need (W.I.N.)

It's not the kind of disease that will kill you. But it certainly will reduce the effectiveness of your efforts. Here is an exercise.

Go back and look at your last 25 cold email messages. How many of them contain sentences like, "I am hoping...", "I would be grateful..." or "We are trying..."? The variations can be many, of course. Let me be crystal clear. The customer does not care about your W.I.N. They care about their own. If you don't like that fact, find a new career. Sales is not about you, and it certainly is not for you.

Fortunately, there is a cure. It's called empathy. If you develop a mindset that you will face your daily selling tasks with the power of empathy, you will attain this vital perspective. Yes, you will begin to view everything through the only lens that matters: that of each prospect and each customer.

The World Is an Increasingly Noisy Place

Gone are the days of the frontier, when crowds were rare, and peace could be found on an isolated patch of ground where the sounds of birds and crickets chirped. These were mostly blissful times in which entertainment was books and stories around a fire. There were eons during which wonders like a meteor shower or eclipse were magical.

Fast forward, and each of us knows that multitasking is the norm; silence is fleeting, and daily demands feel ever more burdensome. Indeed, wondrous discoveries garner painfully short attention. This is the environment in which modern people live daily. There is little time for distraction, and we thrive within time blocks during which disturbances feel like mosquito bites.

So, to defend our sanity, we erect a "force field." It consists not of energy but indifference, apathy, and even disdain. Some days, our force field is the only thing that protects our well-being.

This is the playing field for modern selling. The old-timers (like me) may claim, "Selling is selling. All you need to do is build relationships." While that may be true, the twenty-first century has ushered in incredible technological advances that have led to different buying behavior. Modern code(s) of conduct have hobbled old icebreakers like weekly lunches and relationship opportunities like golf.

THE BUYING JOURNEY HAS CHANGED

There used to be three primary ways to learn about new products and services: events, mail, and salespeople. Some may argue referrals were and are crucial. Of course, they are. All of these are simply introductions to a salesperson or event—at which there are a bunch of salespeople.

Today, we have the Internet in many forms, from websites to social media and communities to e-commerce, with more innovations happening yearly. Yes, the Internet has served to strengthen the buyers' force fields. Behind this protection, folks like you and I have developed a preference for a silent buying journey. We research and plan and shop until our fingers are tired, all the while not letting on that we have an interest.

The salesperson's job is to penetrate the force field. The initial objective is to catch their attention in the hopes of making an appointment or pitch. Salespeople use that same Internet to attempt more cold "touches." Businesses play the numbers game. We used to be capable of a mere couple thousand phone calls per year and maybe a few hundred meetings. Shrinking budgets and the drive to productivity have created a growing belief that handshakes and live, in-person meetings are expensive remnants of a bygone era.

So, we must *do more calls* and *more emails*! Buyers love that.

So, Why Would I Endure This Life?

Some of you are telling yourself, *This guy is full of it. That's not my life. I'm shaking hands regularly.* Well, I'll bet you that those doing so have been in the business for quite some time and have a well-established book of relationships and a strong network ready to refer them. Others think, *Why would I want to be in sales?* Oh, there's a damn good reason. It's gratifying to work so hard, make connections, and help folks fix, accomplish, or avoid something important. Honestly, it's an adrenaline rush, and it is incredibly fulfilling. When the hard work delivers, it's an almost heady feeling that delivers lessons that build new success atop the old. It's exhilarating!

But, to win, you must penetrate the force field. How?

Mail? Who Sends Mail Anymore?

Imagine the early days of mail. You received a letter! You felt special. If you do not remember the joy you felt as a child when the Sears catalog arrived, ask an older person. It was truly joyous. It was time to make our list for Santa.

Then came junk mail. A flurry of catalogs followed in the wake of Sears' success. There were toys and fishing gear, car accessories, and apparel. Oh, the postal workers built their muscles from the weight as it grew with each passing year. So, the perceived value of the catalog waned. Do you still feel that same excitement, like that of a child, when you receive the monthly sale flyer from your warehouse store? Why not? You can spot junk mail easily. You can quickly skim through the mail and sort the junk into the circular file cabinet. It almost feels athletic.

So, no one does mail much anymore. Well, not very well. Can you say, "*Act NOW!* We'll Clean Your Dryer Vents For Free When You Schedule Your Duct Cleaning Before Labor Day"?

Be An Anomaly

So, what is an ambitious salesperson to do? It starts with a new attitude. Examine everything you do in excruciating detail through a new lens. Sit in your prospect's chair and look at the computer screen through their eyes. This is not something that you do once in a while in between doom-dialing to meet your daily phone call quota. This must become your new obsession.

This new attitude demands that you become hyper-observant of what is going on in the world of your prospective fans. What is your mission? Deliver every encounter when they prefer and how they prefer. You simply must become a student of human behavior and the nuances of communication. But be forewarned, as technology changes, so do techniques and skills. You must become an eternal student of what garners attention and what does not. You must be a scientist who experiments, learns, and experiments again. Most important, one must never assume that all people are the same.

Then and only then will you stick out, not like a sore thumb, like a green thumb.

Now that we have that out of the way, let's get down to brass tacks. Let's discuss some examples in which you can become an anomaly in your day-to-day selling activities.

Mail Can Still Work

Raise your hand. How many of you still send greeting cards? In these times when the mail feels like it belongs in the recycling bin, the greeting cards industry continues to grow at a CAGR of 0.9% per year. Yep, I'll bet many of you still keep stamps on hand so that you can send greeting cards. Why? Because greeting cards never end up in the trash, leaving the recipient feeling good about you and your intentions. Greeting cards stand out above the junk mail and are cherished, or at the bare minimum, saved for a time. I know that in our home, we always retain the many birthday and holiday cards we receive for weeks, if not months, after the event.

How can you use greeting cards to help a prospect understand that you genuinely like to connect with people? Oh, you can tell the ones who try to use this technique in a disingenuous manner. Yeah, they use that lame font that they want you to think is handwritten. What a joke. Hello, trash can! But do greeting cards work? I had one fellow keep 7 years of my unique 3D pop-up Christmas cards on his desk. He displayed them year-round. Oh, I'm confident that I had his attention.

How many of you road warriors carry a stack of blank note cards with envelopes? When was the last time that you wrote a handwritten note saying a simple "thank you" to a client? No, not because you want something in return, but because you are simply a nice person. How far do you think that will go toward creating and nurturing a relationship?

I know what you are thinking. If everyone reads this, everyone will do it, and it will stop being an anomaly. Yep, I imagine so. Do you remember what I said about being observant and continuous learning?

Simply put, salespeople will follow trends and fads in the pursuit of doing more, and more, and more. Be an anomaly and do what others do not. Whatever you do, be authentically yourself when you do it. Prospects and customers are people, and people take notice.

COLD EMAIL CAN STILL WORK

You now know you shouldn't begin with "I" or "we." Here's another gem for you:

"I'm just circling back to see if you received my last email."

Have you ever seen that message in your inbox or, hopefully, in your junk folder? It's usually followed by some long diatribe or forwarded message attempting to fool or educate you. Like junk snail mail, we have an incredible talent for spotting SPAM emails a mile away, too. We can skim through it and delete it so fast that we can get into an enjoyable rhythm with our keystrokes. OK, my Uncle Ernie still struggles with SPAM. But we all love him just the same. He's so much fun at family gatherings. But I digress.

What if your email was super short and to the point?

What if it was painfully short?

I assure you, you will be an anomaly. It's easier to skim, read, and digest. It's less work for our brains. It is to the point and tees up an attractive, easily digestible Call To Action. You thought that the K.I.S.S. principle meant something else? In the email world, it means **Keep It Super Short**. Here are some simple guidelines:

- Subject line? Keep It Super Short.
- Make it easy to skim and read on a phone.
- For goodness' sake, why are you trying to "tell" them? Ask a question.
- With that question, demonstrate your insight into their situation.
- Use insights from others to bolster your credibility.
- Don't you dare mention your features.
- CTA? Keep It Super Short.

If you demonstrate insight and ask a question to start a conversation, the interest you will generate will lead to more people executing your CTA. The fewer words you use, the less likely your message will contain SPAMmy language that tips off the junk filters. Forget artificial intelligence; human intelligence is amazing. If your email message is quick and easy to digest and you are not asking for much effort from the recipient, your response rate will be higher. You may find that you receive more negative responses. They're easier for the recipient to send, as well. That's helpful, though. Now you know where not to waste your time or how to improve.

The highest response rate I ever received from one of those damned customer surveys that no one loves and most everyone ignores was titled "The Shortest Survey Ever." To answer your question, it was indeed the shortest ever. No link to some survey form. Just one multiple-choice question. My response rate was north of 30% with simple replies that consisted of one letter: A, B, C, or D. Several folks took the time to thank me for such a unique message. One person told me, "I hate surveys. I only did it because you said it was the shortest ever." Then, like a number of folks, she shared positive feedback about her experience.

No, I didn't use some email blast software. I sent them individually from me. Yes, it took time. But this is a very different approach to a dreaded task. How can you be an anomaly and even make otherwise laborious efforts, dare I say it, fun? Improved outcomes are a thoughtful, creative brainstorm away.

Now, add an animated GIF to your message. Add a clickable link to the video on YouTube. It takes time. It makes them stop and look. It's measurable. It works.

THE LESS CROWDED INBOX

What do you do when your email messages are not returned?

What do you do when Caller ID is your enemy and calls are ignored?

You go to the less crowded inbox. Sometimes, that means simply knocking on the door. Folks, there was a time when cold calling was *the* selling tool. Those who learned how to execute cold calling well were artists. Sadly, technology and societal upheaval have disrupted the cold call, and the costs to execute them well have risen. Now, there are some industries that still rely on cold calls, and I applaud it. But there are legions of salespeople who wouldn't dream of it. They are timid and fear they might offend someone. Well, it is an art, and it takes practice.

There was a time when lobbies were a continual stream of salespeople. Ah, the good old days. My, how I miss you. Heightened security, gatekeepers, remote work, and a preference for independent research have decreased the probability of success. But, have you ever thought, *What do I have to lose?* The sale! Well, that is being rather presumptive. The sale is never guaranteed unless you are accustomed to a 100% close ratio. The lobby is a less crowded inbox.

Good salespeople put themselves in situations that improve their luck. Plan a day, visit the area, and try your luck. Heck, be honest and say so. I thought I'd try my luck." No need to lie. I have had more lunches from this tactic than I can remember. Speaking of lunch, where do the folks go for lunch? That's where I'll be. Yes, I have had impromptu sales calls by placing myself in the right locations and waiting for "luck" to happen. Are the other salespeople there? Not likely. It's a less crowded inbox.

Text messages are a less crowded inbox. Now, be careful. Text messaging is intimate. But Lord knows that folks pay attention to their text messages. They may not answer. But they do read every one. You will be an anomaly if you can negotiate that less-crowded inbox

When was the last time you delivered an important proposal overnight? If a proposal is of high value, isn't it worth the effort to ensure delivery and attention? If a relationship is worth developing, isn't it worth an investment in assuring delivery? Overnight envelopes are placed on chairs and keyboards. They are placed front and center by gatekeepers. The gatekeepers ignore their responsibility to keep the gate when handling overnight packages. A person's chair is the quintessential less crowded inbox.

LinkedIn has become a horrible experience with the advent of the "Pitch Slap". Yes, people hate the tired connect and pitch so much that it has earned its own unique name. So, why would you repeatedly Pitch Slap people on LinkedIn when they hate it so much? After all, LinkedIn is a networking platform. It is a place in which folks frequent to search for a job. They need help. Do you want to be an anomaly on LinkedIn? Simply network with people. Connect regularly with folks in your industry, ask them to meet, and promise them there will be no sales pitch from you. I meet with 4-6 people every single week using a real networking strategy. Offer to help people with their efforts, and don't sell. If you genuinely care, they will learn who you are and what you do and begin to trust you. When and if they are ready, they will call you or refer you. Remember, referrals are crucial! This is just the tip of the iceberg that represents the set of tools available on social media—if you are genuinely empathetic.

BE CREATIVE—AND AN ANOMALY

These examples are a good set of basics to get started. But creativity is infinitely beautiful. Do you think that the only tools that you have available are phone calls, emails, mail, and handshakes? I think not. The anomalous world is full of new ideas and techniques that will lift you above the noise.

Think, brainstorm, and experiment your way into new ways to garner attention so that you can help people. After all, the most fantastic way to be an anomaly is to help first, help often, and help selflessly.

About the Author

Chuck Coxhead's passion for business growth was ignited after leading a remarkable business turnaround. The joy of achieving extraordinary differentiation and creating a new category was so gratifying that he became driven to replicate this success for a new generation of executives and sales and marketing leaders.

Continually saddened by the seemingly endless tales of stalled growth and frustration among entrepreneurs and business leaders, he has invested the entirety of his working hours—and more—to research, learn, experiment, and execute increasingly effective revenue programs.

Using decades of experience as an industrial engineer, seller, marketing, and leader in manufacturing, automation, high technology, information technology, and warehousing, he is focused on helping companies become an anomaly and rise above the competitive noise. It takes a truly aligned team to take risks and create a strategy that continuously seeks to find what works today and what will work tomorrow as the business landscape evolves.

Helping others achieve newfound success is what continues to motivate Chuck every single day to show up and give it his all.

Chuck's motto is "Dream BIG!"

In the Grip of the Unconscious

Carol Putnam, PhD

Humans believe we control our lives and make decisions based on our logical thought processes. We believe that we automatically learn from failures and know why we believe what we believe. We also generate plausible explanations for why we took a specific action, made a particular decision, or felt an emotion.

However, what if I told you that the stimuli that drive our behavior daily result from brain activity we are blind to? What if I told you that 95 percent of our decisions, actions, emotions, and behaviors depend on brain activity beyond our conscious awareness?

Yes, that blob encased in your skull, which represents about 2 percent of your body mass and consumes roughly 20 percent of your body's energy resources, is the culprit. Whether we are diving into our business financials, reviewing SEO data, or writing our goals for the next quarter, the unconscious is churning away.

Below the surface of our awareness, the unconscious reviews all the information your brain is bombarded with every second, recognizing patterns, assigning data into categories, and applying rules. These unconscious rules determine our behavior, but we can't explain them because they are outside our awareness.

The way we vote, the things we purchase and when, the people we hire or don't hire, the information we pay attention to or ignore, the people we move toward, and those we walk away from are determined by heuristics (strategies) created by the unconscious. The unconscious mind dictates how we address the world, approach situations when we feel stuck, and cope with failure.

Why is the unconscious mind so influential in our functioning? Simple, because if we had to consciously think about everything we do before or while doing it, we wouldn't survive as a species. Imagine if you had to consciously think about walking, the muscles that needed to fire in the legs, the movement of your feet, how far to lift each foot, how to balance on one foot, how to place the foot, the space between steps, and on, and on.

Humans have ancient fundamental drives that unconsciously affect our thoughts and actions. What are they? The need to survive, be safe, mate, and cooperate. To act on those drives, our ancestors operated unconsciously. Their brains were making decisions long before there was language and

the ability to communicate intention. These ancestral unconscious needs drive our behavior in this complex, fast-paced,
and information-rich modern world.

Conscious thought is a significant tax on our resources and a
slow process. The unconscious can process vision, sense perception, understand language, recognize faces and emotions,
and make us step back up on the curb so we don't get hit by
the speeding cyclist while consciously pondering what to have
for dinner or our next client call.

Okay, all that is interesting, but what does it have to do with
my ability to run my business effectively? Or better yet, to be
able to be successful in my business? Simple, the more you
understand your unconscious, the more you can utilize it effectively to help you solve problems and make better decisions.

According to Yale psychologist Dr. John Bargh, the brain
operates simultaneously in three distinct time frames: the past,
present, and future. Our thoughts, emotions, and behaviors
result from the unconscious rules within these time frames.

Past: The ancestral deep core needs of safety, security, mating,
and cooperation. Also, what the unconscious learns in the first
twelve months of life (whether the world is safe or unsafe)
and the cultural, societal, and collaboration rules (implicitly
known by age four). There is also the recent past, what hap-
pened within the last hour or two.

Present: What the unconscious is attending to now, e.g., the
room's temperature, what the chair you are sitting on feels
like, whether you are hungry, the light, proximity to others,
ambient sounds, and background conversations. All that happens while concentrating on your marketing strategy.

Future: Our hopes, goals, and intentions. When we set a
goal, the unconscious moves toward the desired outcome. (If

we fix a goal and take no action, the unconscious mind will either nag us or send us negative messages about our worth, etc.) When the unconscious is focused on our goal, it will influence our thoughts, behaviors, and emotions before we are aware of what we are doing or experiencing.

However, be careful what you wish for; the unconscious may create challenges for you. Moving forward on a goal can cause us to operate outside of our values and beliefs about ourselves. It can influence who we become friends with and who we cut loose from our lives. In some ways, our goals can reconfigure who we are.

The **unwelcome news** is that we are governed by our unconscious mind, which has been scanning the environment, collecting data, determining patterns, learning, solving problems, storing memories, and developing rules since birth. We operate from unconscious protocols, automatic thought processes, and habits. We are not in control of the unconscious.

The **good news** is that we can become aware of and accept the reality of the unconscious and learn how to work with and utilize its power to improve our lives and businesses. However, to do so takes intention, practice, and developing specific habits. When you understand how the unconscious operates, you can begin to work with it rather than be frustrated by unfulfilled intentions.

EXERCISES AND PRACTICES THAT CAN HELP YOU WORK WITH YOUR UNCONSCIOUS

These exercises are broader than "How do I grow my business?" or "How do I improve my business?" That is intentional. In my work with executives inside and outside of worldwide corporate environments, managing a business is only one part of their life experience. Our business life is but one aspect of who we are as humans. If your health, relationships, or other aspects of your life function poorly, it will negatively impact your business.

FOUNDATIONAL ACTIONS

OPERATE FROM YOUR VALUES

Identify your top five values. These values are core to who you are as a person. Your values are critical to you and your sense of self. (If you've never done this exercise before, do an internet search for a list of values as a starting point.)

Why identify your values? Because if you aren't operating from your values, your unconscious will nag you or send you negative messages about your self-worth, which is energy-depleting at best.

When you have your list of five values, use either of these two practices to guide your behavior:

1. Set aside ten minutes and ask yourself: "How am I operationalizing my values?" In other words, how are you running your life and business using your values as a guide? Without overthinking the question, start writing your responses. Write quickly without paying attention to grammar, spelling, etc. You don't want to actively engage the brain's executive center.

   Set an alarm and keep writing until the alarm goes off. If you have more to write, continue writing. If you have a problem getting started, write anything that comes to mind, even if it is "I don't know."

   This exercise will give you a sense of how you *are* or *are not* operating from your values. If you are, congratulations! If you aren't, review the sections below to get ideas on how to shift your behavior.

2. Each day, focus on one of your values. When you wake up, think about the selected value. Set alarms throughout the day (four to six); each time the alarm goes off, take thirty seconds and think about the specified value. With practice, your unconscious will take over and direct your focus and efforts in alignment with your core values. Executives who used this process reported feeling more productive and focused.

EXAMINE YOUR BEHAVIOR

If your actions aren't producing the desired result, perhaps you need to evaluate your behavior. This exercise will help determine, "Is my behavior getting me what I want?"

Write a list of goals for your life and your business. It is crucial to include **relationships** (spouse/significant other, family, friends), **health** (exercise, nutrition, sleep, emotional health), **money** (short and long-term goals for your financial health), **personal growth**, **spirituality or belief system**, **community**, and your **business**.

> Example goals: exercise a minimum of three days a week for twenty minutes (walking, swimming, etc.), get seven hours of sleep a night, be responsible with my financial resources or reduce debt, take a class or research/study something that interests me once a quarter, etc.

1. Review your list. Are your behaviors in alignment with your goals? For example, you may have a goal that you exercise regularly, but your only exercise is walking from your desk to the refrigerator. Give yourself some

grace; the objective is to identify those areas where you aren't in alignment, not to beat yourself up.

2. Now, generate one small behavioral step for each of your goals in which your behavior doesn't align with the goal. Hint: The step has to be something you can easily accomplish immediately. The smaller the step, the more likely you are to complete it. When you complete the step, *consciously acknowledge the action*. Make the acknowledgment simple and goofy, like throwing your arms up and yelling, "Yeah!"

   As you accomplish a small step toward your goal, create the next small step. The list is to focus your unconscious. Formulating and completing small steps creates a new behavior that the unconscious won't negate (the unconscious prefers its rules and existing behaviors), and the acknowledgment activates the brain's reward center.

PRACTICE MINDFULNESS

The unconscious mind has access to information, memories, emotions, etc., that you can illuminate by developing practices that increase your self-awareness. Practicing mindfulness techniques is an avenue to allow this knowledge to become more accessible. Here are some examples.

1. The body scan: This technique of focusing on different muscle groups brings your attention to the areas of tension in your body.

2. Attending to your thoughts mindfully: Sit where you won't be disturbed for five minutes. Uncross your arms and legs, feet flat on the floor, sit comfortably upright, close your eyes, and focus on your breathing. There are multiple resources available online; here are two:

Five-minute mindfulness script

Five-minute script to restore attention

3. Five-minute mindfulness expansion: Practice one of the five-minute meditations above (or another of your choice). This time, pay attention to the thoughts, feelings, and perceptions that come into your mind. Notice them without judgment. After you notice one, focus on your breath and let the thought go. The goal is to begin recognizing thoughts and feelings as transitory.

4. Practice curiosity. After a mindfulness practice, be curious about what you experienced for a few minutes. Ask yourself (without judgment), "I wonder what that is about?" or, "I wonder what that is connected to?" When you ask yourself a question from a sense of curiosity and then let it go, the unconscious will go to work to answer it.

PRACTICE KAIZEN

"Kaizen and innovation are the two major strategies people use to create change. Where innovation demands shocking and radical reform, all kaizen asks is that you take small, comfortable steps toward improvement." – Robert Maurer, Ph.D.

The small steps of kaizen defuse the unconscious automatic fear response to significant change. The brain is wired to respond to any new change, challenge, or opportunity by triggering an initial fear response. Using kaizen practices to create change avoids the fear response while building new neural connections in the brain.

The **six kaizen strategies** recommended by Dr. Maurer are:

- Ask small questions to avoid fear and encourage creativity.

- Think small thoughts to develop new skills and habits.
- Take small actions that you can complete.
- Solve small problems even when you are in crisis mode.
- Bestow small rewards.
- Look for and recognize the small but crucial moments that others ignore.

Make your small questions *positive* and *open-ended*. For example:

- What would I be doing differently if I were guaranteed not to fail?
- What is one small step I could take to reach my marketing goal?
- What is one small step I could take immediately to improve my business? What is one small question I could ask another person that would provide me with new insight? What is one small thing about me (or my business) that is special and unique?
- What is one small step I could take to improve my health?

Mind Sculpture

Use this practice to ease into a situation or task you avoid because it makes you uncomfortable. When we think about a challenging task or conversation, the unconscious generates a worst-case scenario and centers our attention on our fear. This exercise focuses the unconscious on **what you want to happen, not what you fear will happen.**

1. Identify a task that makes you feel uncomfortable. Plan to give yourself time to create the new neural networks (a minimum of two weeks if you practice daily).

2. Decide how many seconds you want to devote to this activity each time. Keep the time allotment small, but repeat it multiple times daily so the brain begins to rewire.

3. Select a location in which you won't be disturbed. Sit down and get comfortable. Close your eyes. You are going to create a mental model.

4. Imagine you are in that uncomfortable or challenging situation and are viewing it through your own eyes. (Make sure the imaginary vision is in color and life-size.) What is the setting? (Coffee shop, office, Zoom meeting, etc.) What does the environment look like? Who else is there? What do they look like? What are their facial expressions? What clothing are they wearing? What is their posture? Get as detailed as possible. You are creating this in your mind; there are no mistakes.

5. Now, expand your awareness to all your senses. What are the ambient sounds (the screech of an espresso machine, the whir of air conditioning) in the background? What are the smells (a fresh latte, a scented candle)? What is the temperature in the room? What are your body's physical sensations (relaxed breathing, relaxed facial muscles)?

6. Imagine that you are in that conversation or performing that task. (Don't move; this is a practice in your mind.) What do you say? What does your voice sound like? What is your posture? What are your facial expressions? What are your gestures? What specifically are you doing?

7. Envision a positive response to your conversation or activity. Perhaps imagine the other person leaning forward with a curious look. Maybe they are taking notes and nodding their head, or they ask thoughtful questions. (If so, what are they?)

8. Practice this sequence multiple times a day. It should only take a few minutes. When it has become habitual and automatic, you know your brain has created new neural connections for this activity.

9. Now, imagine the worst-case scenario and how you would respond effectively. Imagine yourself remaining calm, thoughtful, and patient. (What do you look like? How do you sound? What is your breath rate? Etc.) What you want to practice mentally is successfully responding to that worst-case scenario. Don't spend much time on the worst-case scenario; you want to focus your brain on how you respond effectively.

10. When you feel ready, try a few small steps. If the task is a difficult conversation, practice out loud in front of a mirror or a supportive friend, or record your practice session and review it. Before you practice, focus on what you look like, sound like, and feel in your mind sculpture process. You want to continue strengthening the neural connections you have created in your brain.

Now, you are ready to engage in the previously uncomfortable task or conversation with new neural connections and a new focus. (Exercise modified from Dr. Robert Maurer's Kaizen Mind Sculpture process.)

BUILD NEW HABITS EFFECTIVELY

Whether your goal is to begin exercising, focus on your values, or change how you manage your budget, setting the right intentions and cues and creating the right environment is crucial. Here is a process to mindfully set yourself up for success.

1. What is the habit you want to create? Why is it important? How will it improve your goal, business, life, relationship, _____?
2. Identify small steps and build upon those steps as you are successful. (Use your kaizen skills.)
3. What environment will support your new habit? Creating a new habit in the same environment may be more challenging. You may need to identify a place, a chair, etc., to create an environmental cue to trigger and support the change.

   (To change my after-dinner snacking, I had to shift where I sat in the family room.)
4. What is the cue for the new habit? (When I review my schedule for the next day, I will set up my alarms to remind me to focus on my values for thirty seconds.) Make it a formula. "When I do X, then I do Y."
5. Mindfully acknowledge each successful step. Again, you want to trigger the reward center of your brain consciously.

PROBLEM SOLVE USING YOUR UNCONSCIOUS

Conscious cogitation on a problem fatigues the mind. We rarely generate an excellent solution through rumination. If there is a problem you need to solve and you have some time, research the question and get all the facts you need.

Then, set the issue aside mentally and allow your unconscious to go to work. Go for a walk, exercise, meditate, or "sleep on it" overnight. Pay attention to what your unconscious provides;

no matter how "weird" it may be, most likely, it is an idea, metaphor, or image.

If your unconscious wakes you at night, nagging you about a task, goal, or unfinished project, turn on the light and draft a plan to address the issue. In the morning, review the plan and create small steps. The unconscious is excellent at problem-solving but not very good at making specific future plans.

Our conscious and unconscious processes operate at the same time, dynamically, using the same parts of the brain. One is not better than the other; they both have specific functions and influence each other. Conscious experiences may loiter in our minds, unconsciously influencing the following experience (e.g., spilling a cup of coffee on ourselves on the way to a meeting and then not feeling confident or distracted in the ensuing conversation).

Unconscious processes are constantly working on our essential problems and goals and will provide us with insights, solutions, and answers. When we set intentions, the unconscious will direct our attention to things relevant to those goals. At the same time, our external environment provides cues and prompts that can influence our behavior unconsciously.

We are constantly being bombarded with information and cues to influence all aspects of our lives. The more you understand how the unconscious works, the more you can utilize its processes to make better decisions, stay focused on your goals and values, develop new skills, and, most importantly, keep yourself from buying that bag of sour cream and cheddar cheese potato chips.

Mauer, Robert, Ph.D. (2014) One Small Step Can Change Your Life, The Kaizen Way. Workman Publishing Company, New York

ABOUT THE AUHOR

Carol Putnam, Ph.D., is a leadership and executive coach. She helps executives and managers identify and solve their most significant pain points and critical challenges. Working with Carol, leadership teams have transformed from dysfunctional groups to dream teams that dramatically improve the bottom line.

She spent more than 22 years working in global hi-tech corporations in roles where she focused on organizational development, change management, leadership and management development, communication strategy, and executive coaching, always helping organizations become more effective.

Carol helps clients uncover the obstacles and challenges that keep them from achieving their professional and personal goals. A perpetual student of neuroscience, she incorporates the latest research into "brain hacks" she teaches her clients.

Becoming Your
Own Medicine

Dr. Andrea Renee Rivera

This chapter and my life thus forward are dedicated to my mother, who died on March 25, 2023. May my life and all the sacrifices she and my father made on my behalf be justified by the value my life contributes to humanity. I am forever grateful to God, my family, real friends, teachers, and colleagues, without whom I would have already died and would have nothing of value internally or externally to stand on or contribute.

> "People are not disturbed by things,
> but by the views they take of them."
>
> — **Epictetus**, *Enchiridion*

Heath is not a one-size-fits-all lifestyle proposition based on being "active, eating less, and moving more." Health is holistic and demands harmony of mind, body, and spirit. As a personal trainer, yoga instructor, health coach, and acupuncturist, working with many active people who were starving themselves and exercising in ways that caused injuries, I have seen misguided good intentions and blindly following health trends can be as unhealthy as neglect.

We are all called to define our own health success criteria and decide what we are willing to do to be healthy. Just like a vintage classic car, human beings also require decade specific management, maintenance, environment, and use to continue thriving instead of dying. Healthspan, the years we can live without chronic debilitating disease, doesn't have to be limited by our lifespan's chronological conventional age limits when we choose to take responsibility for our human health and performance and learn to live in a way that promotes health, wellbeing, and longevity.

The ancient lifestyle based human health management and performance enhancement technology of Traditional Chinese Medicine (TCM) offers a complete holistic, customized, self-awareness and self-care-based healthcare system resting on 8,000 years of wisdom chronicled in written word over 4,000 years in books like *The Yellow Emperor's Classic of Medicine*. This ancient tech of how to live well outlined in TCM has been clinically researched and utilized successfully by the modern Western healthcare system for treatment of disease conditions including acute and chronic pain, Post Traumatic Stress Disorder (PTSD), fertility, digestive and chronic autoimmune health conditions, as well as superhuman peak performance, and longevity. TCM modalities practiced for thousands of years and shown to be effective by modern clinical research can cut through the noise of short term, unsustainable and counterproductive health trends. The body's self-healing capacity can be activated and sustained by embodying TCM principles and lifestyle-based self-care practices.

Quality of life, health, and longevity can be accessible at any age, despite health history, and regardless of economic status through the use of TCM self-care tools. Internationally renowned TCM based master trainers and healers such as Bruce Frantzis, the foremost Western expert in Wu and Yang style tai chi who has delivered over 10,000 medical chi-gong treatments, and Dr. Roger Jahnke, OMD, Acupuncturist, and world-renowned translator, educator, and author of bestselling books such as *The Healer Within,* practicing Acupuncture and chigong since the 1980's, are living examples of what is possible. Their personal lives and work mentoring thousands of others over decades of time in self-healing TCM practices, shows that health can be achieved and maintained at any age with the simple daily habits of self-regulation practices that don't require any external equipment or modern electronic technology. TCM practices such as Tai Chi, Self-Healing Chigong, meditation and breathwork also known as mindfulness stress reduction practices (MSR) only require time to practice and can achieve superhuman sustainable health results capable of overcoming orthopedic injury, disease diagnoses and reversing chronological aging without resulting in orthopedic injury.

As an acupuncturist with a clinical practice working with over 10,000 patients in clinics since 2013, I have seen that many people can take far better care of their car and house than their health. Many people can also be engaged in what they thought were healthy lifestyle habits that are counterproductive and contributing to injuries and disease. Many patients come to me with health regimens that do not deliver the desired results. Many have been on protocols of diet, supplements, medications, treatments, surgeries, and exercise to treat traumatic injuries or chronic disease conditions for a significant amount of time without evaluating what is a sustainable good fit for lasting results. Overwhelmed and overbooked personally and professionally, patients find it hard to keep up with unrealistic self-care long-term. Growing physical discomfort demands attention when work and play activities become limited by health challenges including resistant weight gain with hormone imbalances, insomnia, anxiety, fatigue, brain fog, and escalating chronic disease conditions. By partnering with patients as diagnosis detectives, helping them uncover the root causes of their discomfort and how they can help themselves with their daily lifestyle habits, patients can become their own medicine and achieve mind-body mastery with a sustainable lifestyle that can produce better health, wellbeing, and longevity.

I didn't know TCM provided a lifestyle handbook for health. I didn't look closely at my lifestyle until chronic pain and long-term health challenges from a severe car accident in 1994 shut my entire life down. Being run down in the street as a pedestrian by a taxicab going forty miles an hour at 23rd St. and Maddison Ave. on my walk home from the NYC subway station offered a 90 percent chance of death and a lifelong chronic pain challenge. I learned that physically, mentally, and emotionally recovering from the accident was not a one to three-year healing process that could be finished but rather a lifelong health management project I cannot escape. Overwork as a passionate and dedicated entrepreneur willing to do "whatever it takes" to establish and grow my businesses has made health management even more challenging.

I offer this chapter as a practical and actionable invitation to become your own medicine. We can grow our health problems or our longevity and peak performance solutions by how we choose to live each day. The first step toward becoming our own medicine and creating better health and longevity is awareness. Taking the time to check ourselves and get clear on what is and is not working for us at least once a year, and ideally every six months can be simple, and effective. I have used an original Four Pillars of Health evaluation model in my clinical practice since 2016. Anyone can use this tool long-term at least once a year to make sure they live in a way that makes them healthier. You can do this Four Pillars of Health evaluation right now. Rate your 1) stress, 2) sleep, 3) diet, and 4) exercise on a scale of zero to ten, with ten being the highest quality and level of satisfaction. Once you are clear on the lowest-score health category, you can commit to the second step of doing a six-week healthy habits challenge on your own or in one of my virtual or live groups to change your behavior to permanently bring up your lowest score.

I have led six-week healthy habits challenges with small groups of six to twelve people since 2008. One of the tricks to making a new healthy habit stick is to attach it to an existing habit you have had for a very long time that you never skip, like lying in bed or brushing your teeth. You can start with one or two healthy habits you add to your lifestyle, such as stretching in bed before or after sleep. Slow and steady additions of one healthy habit at a time consistently over consecutive six-week periods can make healthy habits stick and create a sustainable lifestyle that produces permanent results that can compound with greater benefit over time. The goal is to consistently maintain at least a level seven out of ten in all Four Pillars of Health areas long-term with simple, doable, and practical daily habits you keep doing.

As we age, we can start to notice enough health challenges and discomfort to get motivated to reinvent our lifestyle and learn more about living in a better health-promoting way. However, overwhelming responsibilities, unmanaged stress and unhealthy habits can be challenging to overcome. Permanent change can require professional support such as health and human performance coaching and behavioral psychology therapy for employing techniques such as exposure therapy, neuro-associative conditioning, and cognitive behavioral therapy. These therapies can help with overcoming both outer and inner world challenges and creating a new empowering belief system that can fuel the courage to break through limiting perceptions and the mental and emotional inner turmoil that can block changing patterns of behavior.

Over time, unhealthy habits can be broken by relentless interruption of the old patterns of thoughts, feelings, and behaviors. For example, instead of using opiate foods such as sugar, dairy, chocolate, grains, caffeine, alcohol, or nicotine and other prescription or street drugs with side effects to manage emotions, energy levels, pain, and stress, a person can start to choose other self-regulation tools instead such as breathwork or laughter yoga. Instead of high-impact and high-risk sports for social exercise like jogging, heavy weightlifting, tennis or pickleball, a hike, bike ride, yoga, Pilates, Tai Chi, or Aikido class can be chosen instead.

Daily practices of TCM rooted mindfulness for stress reduction (MSR) including breathwork, Yoga, or meditation practices are available online for free from the HeartMath Institute. These clinically researched practices have been shown to be effective at increasing health and wellbeing. MSR practices offer a way for anyone anywhere to reset the nervous system out of the ridged, emotionally reactive, fight/flight sympathetic nervous system response that shuts down creativity, immunity, regeneration, and digestion. MSR practices used as needed throughout the day can shift the body immediately out of the disease promoting sympathetic nervous system response into the ideal parasympathetic healing nervous system response that promotes health, well-being, creativity, fulfilling connection, and longevity.

Daily lymphatic drainage stimulation is another cornerstone of mind-body mastery that can lead to peak performance, health, and longevity. Lymphatic drainage can be understood as how the garbage of toxic chemicals from air, water, food, medications, and waste products from physiological chemical reactions, digestion, regeneration, and repair is cleared out of our body's neighborhood. Lymphatic drainage stimulating practices can be done in minutes. For example, the TCM chigong warm-up of body tapping can be done by tapping a soft fist all over the body as self-massage acupressure followed by bouncing up and down by flexing the knees and ankles and shaking out arms and legs for tension relief. When lymphatic drainage is activated proper circulation of blood, oxygen, nutrients, electricity, and body fluids can be promoted that support internal organ function, producing the correct amounts of energy and hormones to drive regeneration and overall health, longevity, quality of life, and vitality. Receiving anti-inflammatory, circulation promoting, and endorphin producing pain and stress relieving treatments like acupuncture with lymphatic drainage stimulating acupressure massage and regular physical exercise like jumping on a rebounder trampoline just five to 20 minutes a day can, not only clear the garbage out of our body's neighborhood, but also elevate mood and increase energy, mental clarity, memory, and creativity.

Personally, I was naïve and ignorant about how to manage my health and did a lot of things wrong for fifteen years during my first business experience of entrepreneurship from 1992 to 2007. Especially during financial crisis post 9/11, I overworked and exasperated my chronic pain. When my health was at its worst in 2007, I was afraid I would never be healthy again. I thought I could benefit my family more dead than alive, like the *It's a Wonderful Life* movie character George Bailey believed. I tried to kill myself three times. So, I am here to tell you the whole truth about what I did wrong and the results that can come from unmanaged stress, fear-based thinking and putting work and money before health and relationships. In my experience, putting work and money first led to bad decision making, and ultimately resulted in the divorce, bankruptcy, and the dissolution of my first business I was desperately trying to avoid through overwork.

The foundation of health and peak performance in life and work can be seen as stress management. Self-awareness and employing self-regulation to reset our state of being despite challenging circumstances is mind-body mastery. Noticing we are in a stressed sympathetic nervous system fight/flight state that is emotionally reactive and physically tense and acting immediately to change our state back to the parasympathetic, relaxed, reasonable, and present state of being ASAP is necessary for better decision making, health and peak performance. Mind-body mastery is being able to self-regulate our nervous system out of the fight/flight state in a short amount of time *no matter what.*

Our health rests on the resiliency of our nervous system. When we have weathered trauma in life, we can develop post-traumatic stress disorder (PTSD) that can require the consistent long-term use of mindfulness stress reduction practices (MSR) in response to any triggering new stressful events. Breathing techniques like inhaling to the count of four, holding our breath to the count of seven, and exhaling to the count of eight can help manage stress, PTSD and getting stuck in a stress response. MSR practices along with treatments like acupuncture can help regulate the nervous system and get back command over our mind and emotions, enabling us to preserve our health, well-being, and better problem-solving abilities.

This is not to say that the goal is to avoid feeling and expressing human emotions. On the contrary, holistic health rests on the courage to confront by choice the suffering and difficulties of life's challenging circumstances, feel the painful and over-whelming emotions that are the natural human reaction to perceived threats, and then transmute them, using them as energy and motivation to practice healthy lifestyle habits and let them go. This is the purpose of behavioral psychology's exposure therapy modality. When we choose to face a challenge like facing painful emotions and difficult circumstances, rather than avoiding dealing with them, we experience a completely different neurological and physiological response in our mind and body that can promote the courage, strength, and resiliency we all want and need to be holistically healthy.

In his book *The Feeling is the Secret*, Neville Goddard rec-ommends a time limited emotional release perspective reprograming practice: "If you must explode, get it off of your chest and then reframe it." The modern behavioral psy-chology technique of neuro-associative conditioning, also referred to as "reframing," is a practical and effective way to process and release perspectives and emotions. Reframing can be applied both in the moment of emotional reactivity to a current challenge and past unresolved challenges. Dr. Jordan Peterson's self-authoring program and the work of Byron Katie are written practices of reframing neuro-associative condi-tioning. By using introspective writing tools like these, past and current mental and emotional trauma can be resolved as needed to prevent stress, physical disease escalation and poor emotionally reactive fear-based decision-making under duress that many people regret in hindsight.

The perspective on our lives we choose and the attitude and emotions we embody drive our behaviors each day and can make or break our quality-of-life experience, health, longev-ity, and performance. We can all complain and make excuses about how age, circumstances, or past challenges are prevent-ing us from being healthy. Or we can focus on what we can control and do each day to create better health, well-being, and performance. We can choose to be more aware and take control of how we live. It is possible to strive to become a Jedi-like superhuman mind-body master. We can choose to learn to how to become our own medicine.

References:

Epictetus. (1865). *The works of Epictetus; Consisting of his discourses in four books, The Enchiridion and fragments.* (E. Carter & T. W. Higginson, Trans.). Little, Brown, and Co. https://doi.org/10.1037/12218-000

Frantzis, B. (2023, January 1). *Bruce Frantzis Energy Arts Training Center.* Retrieved August 17, 2023, from https://www.energyarts.com/about/

Jahnke, R. (1998). *The Healer Within: Using Traditional Chinese Techniques to Release Your Body's Own Medicine.* Harper One

Huangdi, a. 2. B., & Veith, I. (1972). *The Yellow Emperor's classic of internal medicine. Chapters 1-34.* New ed. Berkeley; London (2 Brook St., W1Y 1AA), University of California Press.

Stephens I. (2017). Medical Yoga Therapy. *Children (Basel, Switzerland)*, *4*(2), 12. https://doi.org/10.3390/children4020012

HeartMath Institute, a Nonprofit Organization (2023, January 1). *HeartMath Institute, a Nonprofit Organization.* Retrieved August 17, 2023, from https://www.heartmath.org/

Goddard, N. (2023, January 1). *Feeling is the Secret, Neville Goddard.* Retrieved August 17, 2023, from https://www.feelingisthesecret.org/

Katie, B. (2023, January 1). *The Work of Byron Katie*. Retrieved August 17, 2023, from https://thework.com/

Peterson, J. B. (2023, January 1). *The Self Authoring Suite*. Retrieved August 17, 2023, from https://www.selfauthoring.com/

About the Author

From 1992-2007 Dr. Andrea Renee, DACM, LAc. enjoyed 15 years of international acclaim as the president and founder of Andrea Renee, Inc., an innovative Jewelry design and manufacturing house based in SOHO NYC. Her collection was carried in the top global department stores, including Barney's NY & Japan, Daimaru Japan, Fortunoff, Bloomingdales, Macy's, and Nordstrom, as well as her own SOHO NYC boutique with celebrity clients including Drew Barrymore, Johnny Depp, and Julianne Moore. She enjoyed recognition as one of New York Magazine's "favorite downtown jewelry designers" and was featured as her company spokesperson in media coverage, including NY Times, NY Magazine, In Style, Entertainment Weekly, Seventeen, Elle, Cosmo & Savvy Japan, NY Post, Time Out, and Good Day NY.

Since 2007 she has worked with over 10,000 clients. As a certified Yoga and Meditation Instructor since 2007 as well as being a certified Passion Test for Life & Business facilitator she helps entrepreneurs and professionals create work-life balance and legacy. As a Doctor of Acupuncture and Chinese Medicine, Dr. Andrea has extensive training and clinical experience practicing in CA & CO, utilizing East-West integrative, functional, and preventative medicine with nutrition, acupressure massage, energy work, and herbal medicine for resiliency.

The Entrepreneurial Hero's Journey

Eric Rosen

As a master hypnotherapist and executive coach, I've guided many individuals on their journeys to self-mastery. One of the most profound transformations I've witnessed is the Entrepreneurial Hero's Journey (EHJ). Allow me to share the essence of this journey through the stories of two remarkable individuals, Timmy and Jenny. Each is a composite of several of my clients (for privacy and exposition).

Timmy and Jenny, though different in many ways, embarked on similar paths to self-discovery and success. Their stories are filled with challenges, triumphs, and profound insights that reflect the stages of the EHJ. But before we delve into their unique journeys, let's explore the foundational framework that underpins their experiences: Campbell's Hero's Journey (CHJ).

WHAT IS THE HERO'S JOURNEY?

Professor Joseph Campbell was a renowned scholar and mythologist who discovered a universal pattern in stories from different cultures and times. He called this pattern the Hero's Journey (CHJ), a narrative structure that reflects the human experience's spiritual essence. It's a story of adventure, transformation, and self-discovery that resonates with all of us. From ancient myths to modern blockbusters like *Star Wars*, the CHJ captures the imagination and speaks to the soul.

The CHJ is not just a literary device but a mirror reflecting our lives, dreams, fears, and triumphs. It's a path that leads us through challenges and victories, guiding us toward our true selves. It's a spiritual quest transcending time and space, connecting us with the universal human experience.

THE IMPORTANCE OF UNDERSTANDING THE ENTREPRENEURIAL HERO'S JOURNEY (EHJ)

Why should entrepreneurs and business leaders care about the EHJ? This adaptation of Campbell's Hero's Journey is a practical guide to entrepreneurs' unique spiritual and personal growth journey. Here's why a conscious understanding of the EHJ is vital:

- **Personal Growth and Transformation:** The EHJ outlines stages of personal development, from childhood to midlife to self-mastery as a venerated elder and beyond.
- **Business Success and Fulfillment:** Aligning with the EHJ helps you connect business goals with your true self, fostering financial success and spiritual fulfillment.

- **Overcoming Challenges:** Awareness of the EHJ can help you transform setbacks into strength, recognizing challenges as growth opportunities that build resilience.

- **Holistic Approach to Entrepreneurship:** Beyond business strategies, embracing the EHJ promotes a balanced entrepreneurial life, encompassing growth, relationships, and spirituality.

- **Legacy and Impact:** The EHJ emphasizes fulfilling your purpose in service of a greater good so you can build a meaningful legacy.

- **Connection to the Universal Human Experience:** Linking entrepreneurship to universal growth themes, the EHJ underscores that it's not just a career but a profound spiritual journey of transformation borne out of self-mastery.

AN IN-DEPTH LOOK AT THE EHJ

For starters, it helps to appreciate how the EHJ maps to the CHJ. Equipped with these parallels, we'll examine each of the stages of the EHJ in more depth:

Campbell's Hero's Journey (CHJ)	Entrepreneurial Hero's Journey (EHJ)
The Ordinary World	Childhood: Formation of the Core Identity Belief
The Call to Adventure	Adolescence: Beginning of Self-Fulfilling Prophecies
Refusal of the Call	Early Adulthood: Intensification of Self-Fulfilling Prophecies
Trials and Tribulations	Adulthood: Deepening of Self-Fulfilling Prophecies

Campbell's Hero's Journey (CHJ)	Entrepreneurial Hero's Journey (EHJ)
The Abyss	Midlife Crisis: Spiritual Awakening, Need for Transformation
Transformation	Transformation: Self-Mastery Takes Root
Reintegration and Mastery	Reintegration and Mastery: Applying Transformation, Redefining Success
The Return	Venerated Elder: Wisdom, Influence, Authentic Living
Master of Two Worlds (Inner and Outer)	Legacy: Giving Back, Lasting Impact

CHILDHOOD: FORMATION OF THE CORE IDENTITY BELIEF

In this stage, core beliefs about oneself are formed through early experiences and interactions with family, caregivers, and peers. These unconscious beliefs become the foundation of self-image, shaping future behaviors and decisions.

Several psychological theories align with this concept. Sigmund Freud's theory emphasizes unconscious drives from birth in shaping identity.

John Bowlby's attachment theory shows early caregiver relationships influence self-concept before conscious reasoning develops.

Jean Piaget's theory describes the evolution of children's thinking, suggesting early formation of self-beliefs.

These theories collectively support that early experiences and unconscious processes shape identity before whole conscious reasoning has any say.

The entrepreneur struggling to go out on their own might unconsciously fight a belief like *I'm not good enough,* unaware that it's changeable. Subtle, unconscious belief drives self-fulfilling prophecies. Childhood sets the stage for adolescence; adolescence feeds early adulthood, and so on through the midlife crisis.

ADOLESCENCE: BEGINNING OF SELF-FULFILLING PROPHECIES

Overview: Transition to adolescence, where the core identity belief starts to manifest in behaviors and relationships, setting the stage for self-fulfilling prophecies in the form of future challenges.

During adolescence, individuals reinforce their core identity beliefs with persistent patterns of behavior, which make for self-fulfilling prophecies.

Timmy's Journey: "I am not good enough."

Timmy's adolescence is marked by a struggle to prove himself, driven by the belief that he's not good enough.

- **School Performance:** Obsessed with grades, Timmy sacrifices friendships and hobbies for study. Despite achievements, he never feels satisfied, fearing failure.
- **Sports:** Timmy pushes himself to the limit on the basketball team, playing through pain. A missed shot or lost game becomes a personal failure, reinforcing his belief.
- **Relationships:** Timmy avoids asking his crush to the dance, fearing rejection. He believes he's not good enough for her, and his belief becomes a self-fulfilling prophecy, leaving him alone and unfulfilled.

Jenny's Journey: "I am unlovable."

Jenny's core belief that she's unlovable profoundly shapes her adolescence.

- **Friendships:** Jenny struggles to form close friendships, keeping people at a distance. Friends drift away, reinforcing her belief.
- **Family:** Jenny's strained family relationships lead her to withdraw from gatherings, interpreting slights as proof of being unlovable, creating a self-fulfilling prophecy.
- **First Love:** Jenny falls for a classmate but never shares her feelings, believing he could never love her. He starts dating someone else, reinforcing her belief.

EARLY ADULTHOOD: INTENSIFICATION OF SELF-FULFILLING PROPHECIES

Overview: Struggle to reconcile the true self with external expectations, leading to inner conflicts and poor balance across career, health and fitness, and relationships. Personal growth, family, and spirituality.

Timmy's Journey: "I am not good enough."

Timmy's belief that he's not good enough shapes his young adulthood with more significant consequences.

- **Career Choices:** Timmy chooses a demanding finance career to prove his worth, working long hours at the cost of his personal life and health. Despite the success, he fears failure and secretly nurtures his passion for tech innovation as a hobby, not a profession.
- **Romantic Relationships:** Timmy's fear of inadequacy makes him avoid commitment, keeping relationships

superficial. This self-fulfilling prophecy results in loneliness.

- **Personal Development:** Timmy's perfectionism causes him to neglect personal growth, becoming defined by his career. His dissatisfaction reinforces his belief, trapping him in a spiral.

Jenny's Journey: "I am unlovable."

Jenny's belief that she's unlovable intensifies during young adulthood, affecting her life profoundly.

- **Career Relationships:** Jenny avoids networking and collaboration, fearing rejection. Her career stagnates, reinforcing her belief. She continues writing fiction as a hobby, doubting its viability as a career.

- **Romantic Partnerships:** Jenny's fear of abandonment leads to insecure relationships and breakups, confirming her belief.

- **Social Life:** Jenny keeps people at a distance, avoiding social gatherings. Her isolation reinforces her belief, leaving her feeling alone.

Through Timmy's and Jenny's experiences, we see the intensification of the self-fulfilling prophecies from adolescence, now with more significant consequences in their careers, relationships, and personal lives.

ADULTHOOD: DEEPENING OF SELF-FULFILLING PROPHECIES

Overview: Phase of personal and professional challenges where imbalances across different areas of life become more pronounced, as self-fulfilling prophecies owing to the unaddressed core identity belief persist.

Timmy's Journey: "I am not good enough."

As Timmy reaches adulthood, the belief that he's not good enough becomes deeply ingrained, affecting various aspects of his life.

- **Career Burnout:** Despite professional success, Timmy feels inadequate, leading to burnout and health issues. Fear keeps him trapped in his career.
- **Failed Relationships:** Timmy's fear prevents deep connections, resulting in failed relationships and loneliness, reinforcing his belief.
- **Parenting Challenges:** Timmy projects his insecurities onto his children, pushing them to succeed. The pressure strains relationships and confirms his fear of inadequacy.

Jenny's Journey: "I am unlovable."

Jenny's belief that she's unlovable reaches a critical point during adulthood, with far-reaching consequences.

- **Stagnant Career:** Jenny's fear of rejection continues to hinder her career. She avoids leadership roles and opportunities for advancement, leading to a stagnant career that reinforces her belief of being unlovable.
- **Unfulfilling Relationships:** Her fear leads to unsuitable partners and heartbreak, confirming her belief of being unlovable.
- **Parenting Struggles:** Jenny's belief affects her parenting, causing overprotectiveness and strained relationships with her children.
- **Social Isolation:** Her fear of rejection results in withdrawal from friends, leading to isolation that confirms her belief.

Through Timmy's and Jenny's adulthood, the self-fulfilling prophecies deepen, affecting their careers, relationships, parenting, and social lives in complex and painful ways.

MIDLIFE CRISIS: CULMINATION OF SELF-FULFILLING PROPHECIES

Overview: This critical juncture is where the imbalances become insufferable, and a desperate call for a profound transformation must be made or perish.

Timmy's Journey: "I am not good enough."

Timmy's belief reaches a crescendo during his midlife crisis, leading to a series of dramatic events:

- **Career Collapse:** Timmy hits the wall. His health fails, and he loses his job, feeling more inadequate than ever.
- **Marital Breakdown:** A painful divorce and inability to connect reinforce his beliefs of inadequacy.
- **Estrangement from Children:** Timmy's strained relationship with his children reaches a breaking point. His children's resentment confirms his worst fears.
- **Personal Reckoning:** Timmy seeks an intervention of a holistic healing nature, beginning a journey of self-discovery that will finally challenge his core identity belief.

Jenny's Journey: "I am unlovable."

Jenny's belief that she's unlovable leads to a profound midlife crisis:

- **Career Loss:** Stagnation turns to job loss, reinforcing her whole system of beliefs.

- **Relationship Failure:** A painful breakup confirms her core belief.
- **Children's Rebellion:** Motherly smothering leads to strained relationships, intensifying her belief.
- **Social Withdrawal:** Her isolation deepens, leading to depression.
- **Awakening and Transformation:** Jenny pursues personal coaching and healing of her inner child. She begins a journey of self-love and acceptance, finally challenging her core beliefs.

The Midlife Crisis stage is a culmination of self-fulfilling prophecies for Timmy and Jenny, manifesting in crisis but also offering opportunities for profound transformation.

Transformation: Self-Mastery Takes Root

Overview: Emergence from a midlife crisis, free of emotional baggage with limiting beliefs, replaced by a strong self-image fueling a new life trajectory of purpose and possibility.

Timmy's and Jenny's Transformations:

Timmy and Jenny undergo the transformative process described in the 9 Steps to Transformation section. In short, they emerge from their midlife crises with renewed purpose and expanded possibilities. Though different, their journeys follow a similar progression that leads them to a place of self-mastery and empowerment. The profound inner changes they make are reflected in their actions, relationships, and life trajectories.

Reintegration and Mastery: Applying Transformation, Redefining Success

Overview: Phase of applying the newfound self-mastery, redefining success on personal terms, and integrating the transformation into daily life, relationships, and career.

Timmy's Reintegration and Mastery:

- **Embracing Self:** Timmy's transformation drives his creativity and ambition, leading him to establish his tech lab, a dream long suppressed.
- **Redefining Success:** Success for Timmy now means innovation and impact. His tech lab becomes a hub for cutting-edge projects, attracting talented collaborators.
- **Transformed Professional Relationships:** Timmy's leadership style evolves, reflecting his authentic self and fostering a collaborative work environment.
- **Applying Self-Mastery:** Timmy starts making bold decisions, pursuing disruptive technologies, and securing significant investments for his lab.
- **Living with Purpose and Joy:** Timmy's work is filled with purpose and joy, leading to groundbreaking tech achievements.
- **Family Thaw**: Timmy's children notice a change in his energy, and he finds the work-life balance needed to support their growth.

Jenny's Reintegration and Mastery:

- **Embracing Self:** Jenny publishes her first novel, confirming her transformation.
- **Redefining Success:** Success for Jenny means writing that resonates with her authentic self. Her novel receives critical acclaim, reflecting her unique voice.

- **Transformed Literary Relationships:** Relationships with writers and readers deepen, mirroring her growth.

- **Applying Self-Mastery:** Jenny explores new genres and collaborates with renowned authors, expanding her literary influence.

- **Living with Purpose and Joy:** Jenny's writing becomes a source of fulfillment as she continues to express her transformed self through her literary works.

- **Family Reproachment:** With "I'm unlovable" gone from her cosmology, Jenny can reconnect with her children and enjoy quality time with them.

VENERATED ELDER: WISDOM, INFLUENCE, AUTHENTIC LIVING

Overview: Continued cultivation of self-mastery, operating from true identity, spiritual and material rewards deepen and expand.

Timmy's Venerated Elder Stage:

- **Wisdom in Leadership:** Timmy's lab evolves into an industry leader. He becomes a venerated figure in technology, sharing his wisdom mainly through mentorship.

- **Global Influence in Innovation:** His technologies revolutionize healthcare and renewable energy sectors.

- **Authentic Living:** Timmy's work aligns with his true identity, fostering a culture of integrity and innovation.

- **Spiritual and Material Rewards:** Timmy's innovations earn recognition and financial success, mirroring his spiritual growth.

- **Expanding Impact:** Timmy collaborates with governments and organizations to drive technological advancements for societal benefit.

Jenny's Venerated Elder Stage:

- **Wisdom in Literary Leadership:** Jenny mentors young writers, influencing literary trends with her unique voice.
- **Influence in Writing:** Her works become essential reading, sparking cultural dialogs and inspiring a new generation.
- **Authentic Living:** Jenny's writing reflects her true identity, resonating with readers. She lives authentically in her literary pursuits.
- **Spiritual and Material Rewards:** Her works become bestsellers, winning awards and providing financial and spiritual fulfillment.
- **Expanding Impact:** Jenny uses her literary success for philanthropy and advocacy, positively impacting society.

Legacy: Giving Back, Lasting Impact

Overview: Culmination of the good works that come out of Transformation, Reintegration, Mastery, and the Venerated Elder stages where others are empowered to carry on the entrepreneur's legacy and serve the greater good.

Timmy's Legacy Stage:

- **Tech Education Foundation:** Timmy creates a foundation for educating future tech innovators, offering scholarships and mentorship.
- **Global Tech Impact:** His technologies transform industries, shaping ethical, sustainable development policies.
- **Lasting Impact in Technology:** Timmy's legacy inspires future tech leaders through innovation and education.
- **Empowering Others:** His leadership fosters a culture of innovation and integrity, transcending his involvement.
- **Serving the Greater Good:** Timmy's work improves lives, and his foundation nurtures innovators committed to societal change.

Jenny's Legacy Stage:

- **Literary Foundation:** Jenny established a foundation to support new writers with grants, workshops, and publishing opportunities.
- **Global Literary Influence:** Her writing becomes part of curricula, inspiring critical cultural conversations.
- **Lasting Impact in Literature:** Jenny's works become classics, and her foundation nurtures future influential writers.
- **Empowering Others:** Her mentorship fosters creativity and authenticity, empowering others to find their voices.
- **Serving the Greater Good:** Jenny's foundation supports the literary arts, enriching cultural heritage and encouraging thoughtful discourse.

9 Steps to Transformation

Timmy and Jenny came to me as one-on-one clients. Their programs of transformation followed these nine steps:

1. **Dissolving Resistance:** The journey begins with eliminating unconscious resistance to profound changes, opening the path to an Awesome New Reality. This step dissolves the default resistance, paving the way for transformation.

2. **Emotional Cleansing:** Anger and sadness are eliminated, clearing emotional baggage that has long hindered growth.

3. **Uncovering Core Identity Belief:** Using hypnotic regression cast as a four-act play, the core identity belief is uncovered word-for-word, revealing the root of the problem.

4. **Further Emotional Cleansing:** Fear, hurt, guilt, and shame are eliminated, further cleansing the emotional landscape.

5. **Eliminating the Belief:** The core identity belief and the decision to hold it are eradicated, breaking free from thc past.

6. **Anxiety Removal:** If any anxiety remains (unlikely), it is eliminated, ensuring a clear path forward.

7. **Installing New Belief:** A new empowering core identity belief reflects the transformed self and aligns with their empowered life values.

8. **Goal Setting and Visualization:** With complete congruency between conscious and unconscious minds established, a powerful hypnotic visualization follows with a firm date for the goal's fulfillment.

9. **Accountability and Action:** Individuals are held accountable for actions that ratify their profound

inner changes, allowing them to embark on the second half of their EHJ with self-mastery taking firm root.

LOOKING AHEAD ON YOUR ENTREPRENEURIAL HERO'S JOURNEY

- **What if I don't recognize my core identity belief?** Recognizing core identity beliefs may require introspection, therapy, or guidance from a mentor. It's uncovering hidden truths, appreciating how they have shaped your life, releasing the bonds such truths have held, and embracing a new self-image and belief system.
- **What if the challenges seem insurmountable?** Challenges may seem overwhelming; however, they are part of the growth process. Seeking support, embracing the journey, and believing in the potential for transformation will likely lead to breakthroughs.

COMING FULL CIRCLE

Once lost in the maze of self-doubt and confusion, Timmy and Jenny found their paths illuminated by the Entrepreneurial Hero's Journey. They embraced the challenges, transformed their beliefs, and built legacies that transcended mere business success. Most importantly, their family relationships deepened after their midlife crises lifted. Their stories, a testament to the power of inner transformation, inspire others to embark on their journeys.

As I reflect on the transformative journeys of Timmy and Jenny, a profound realization settles in. The Entrepreneurial Hero's Journey is not just a theoretical construct; it's a living, breathing roadmap that resonates with the universal human experience. It's a path that can lead to business success and a life enriched with purpose, authenticity, fulfillment, and wonder.

CONCLUSION

The Entrepreneurial Hero's Journey is far more than a business strategy; it's a spiritual quest that challenges and nurtures the soul. Whether you're just starting or you are a seasoned business leader, insights from the EHJ can lead you toward a path of authenticity, success, and lasting impact if you are open to doing the transformational work at the unconscious level (which is where the soul is in regular contact). Embrace the journey, for it's not just about reaching a destination; it's about discovering who you are and what you are meant to become.

ABOUT THE AUTHOR

Eric Rosen is a fourth-generation American from Brooklyn, NY. Raised in the milieu of reform Judaism, his upbringing was secular, with a curiosity for other cultures. By 18, he had traveled to several holy cities. His journey has been about self-discovery, reinvention, and answering, "Is this all there is?"

Bullied as a child, he discovered later that he is a high-functioning non-neurotypical. Blessed with entrepreneurial instincts, his well-meaning family convinced him to seek out security instead. Always the round peg in square holes resulted in three different careers and frustration. A midlife crisis to find the right livelihood amid obesity, back pain, depression, and sleep apnea led Eric to overcome them all as he found his true calling: hypnosis.

While Eric launched his weight loss practice in 2012, he soon found his forte: releasing emotional baggage and limiting beliefs like "I'm not good enough" and "I'm unlovable." Next, Eric dove into Hawaiian Huna, energy, and the Higher Self to help his clients heal even faster.

Today, Eric coaches leaders to replace self-doubt with unshakeable confidence and break through their barriers. His passions include Pilates, bodybuilding, saunas, and Tibetan throat singing. Eric is the author of the book *Change the One Belief.*

We Don't Buy Products. We Buy Brands!

Fritz Colinet

This world is filled with options. A simple yet profound truth separates the thriving from the struggling: "We don't buy products. We buy brands!" This statement isn't just a catchy phrase; it's a compass that guides businesses or personalities toward success in the complex landscape of consumer behavior.

Imagine you're walking through a supermarket aisle, eyeing a range of similar products. What's that one thing that makes you reach for a particular item? It's not just the physical attributes or the price tag; it's the brand. The promise, the story, and the emotions you have associated with that brand prompt your decision.

BRANDS AREN'T JUST LOGOS – THEY'RE EXPERIENCES

We understand that a brand is more than a logo or a product. It's an experience. The unique identity speaks to consumers, resonating with their values, aspirations, and emotions. Brands aren't confined to shelves; they're etched into the hearts and minds of consumers.

Think about your favorite product, personality, or service. Chances are, there's more than one brand offering something similar. Yet, you're drawn to a particular one. Why? It's because that brand has crafted a narrative that aligns with your lifestyle and aspirations. It's the feeling of familiarity and aspiration that attracts you.

THE SOLID FOUNDATION OF BRAND LOYALTY

Beyond transactions, brands build relationships. Let me say that again: **brands build relationships.** They cultivate loyalty that goes beyond mere sales. A brand that resonates becomes a part of a consumer's journey. It's the reason why someone chooses a specific business coach or a product time and again.

The journey from being a passerby to a loyal customer is paved with trust, authenticity, and a sense of belonging. This is where branding enters the spotlight. I have crafted brand identities that transcend visual aesthetics and delve into the core of a business, understanding its values, essence, and unique proposition.

Branding is the art of turning your identity into a connection. It's about forging emotional bonds that withstand trends. A strong brand isn't just recognized; it's remembered. It's why certain logos evoke smiles, excitement, or a sense of nostalgia, and others don't.

Branding has emerged as the driving force behind professional and business success. Being proficient in your field is no longer sufficient; a solid personal brand sets you apart and opens doors to new opportunities. I am a professional marketer, strategist, brand developer, and creative director with over two decades of experience in the industry. I have successfully helped build over 150 brands and created countless advertising campaigns that have left a lasting impact in their respective markets. I will help you go from obscurity to visibility with my process of building a powerful personal brand that will resonate with your target audience and elevate your presence in the digital world.

Personal branding has evolved into a critical aspect of professional success. I firmly believe it can be a transformative journey for individuals seeking to make a meaningful impact in their chosen ecosystem. Throughout my career, I have witnessed firsthand the immense potential of personal branding. I am committed to sharing my knowledge and insights to help you unlock the full power of your unique qualities and abilities.

CRAFTING A BRAND WITH INTENT

Building your brand is crafting with intent. Your personal brand is how you want people to see you. It's about visibility and the values you outwardly project.

My approach to personal branding revolves around authenticity and strategic thinking. It's not a one-size-fits-all process; it's a tailored journey that caters to the individual aspirations of each person. Whether you're an aspiring musician, solo entrepreneur, business coach, influencer, actor, politician, seasoned professional aiming to scale new heights, or a visionary artist seeking to carve your niche, I'm here to guide you at every step.

The Building Blocks

Let's start and jump into the foundational steps of crafting your powerful personal brand. These steps aren't just theories; they're actionable strategies that will help propel you toward a powerful brand.

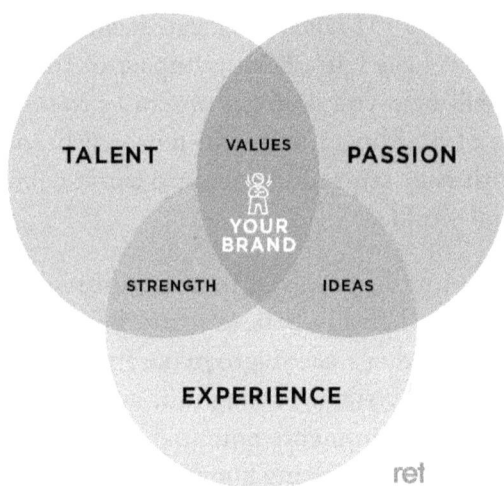

Begin with the EIM (End In Mind)

Step 1: Discover what makes, well, *you*! (Referred to as unique value proposition, or UVP)

Your brand begins with self-discovery. Deep dive into your passions, strengths, and experiences to identify your unique value proposition. What makes you stand out in your industry? Unearth your skills and attributes that resonate with your target audience. Remember, authenticity is critical to building a powerful personal brand.

Why Your Unique Value Proposition Matters:

- **Differentiation:** In a crowded digital space, your UVP is your beacon of differentiation. It communicates why you're unique and why people should choose you over others.

- **Relevance:** A well-defined UVP resonates with your audience's needs, capturing their attention and making your brand more relevant.

- **Memorability:** A concise, impactful UVP is memorable. It sticks in the minds of your audience, increasing the likelihood of them remembering you.

- **Credibility:** A strong UVP backed by your skills and experiences builds credibility and trust. It shows that you're not just making empty claims.

- **Attraction:** When your UVP aligns with what your audience is searching for, it naturally attracts them to your brand. They see you as the solution to their needs.

Your UVP should be aspirational yet influential—a statement that captures the essence of what you offer. It should answer the following:

- What drives you?
- What skills or talents are you most proud of?
- Ask seven people what they like about you.
- Ask the same seven people: "What's my superpower?"
- Write your mission statement for your life.
- What specific value do you bring to your audience?
- How does your expertise solve their pain points or fulfill their desires?
- What sets you apart from others in your field?

Defining your unique value proposition is like discovering your brand's North Star—a guiding light that keeps your brand focused, authentic, and resonant. Once you've discovered it, every aspect of your brand, from your messaging to your visual identity, should have the DNA of your unique value proposition. Your UVP is your brand's soul.

Step 2: Define Your Target Audience

Understanding your target audience is essential in crafting a brand that connects with the right people. Conduct thorough research to identify your ideal audience's needs, preferences, and pain points. This knowledge will help you tailor your brand message and content in a way that resonates with your audience on a personal level. The more you understand your audience's needs, the more targeted you will be.

More Than Demographics

When defining your target audience, you must go beyond standard demographics. While age, gender, location, and income play a role, they don't provide the whole picture. To create a personal brand that truly connects, you need to delve into the psychographics of your audience—understand their motivations, behaviors, interests, and pain points.

Step 3: Shape Your Brand Story

Every great brand has a story. Don't be afraid to share your journey, the challenges you've faced, the challenges you will face, and the victories you've achieved. A compelling brand story creates an emotional bond with your audience, making them more likely to remember and engage with your brand. A great brand story is memorable.

Steps to Craft Your Captivating Brand Story

1. Define your message.
2. Identify key moments.
3. Highlight your core values.
4. Paint a vivid picture with your words.

5. Understand your audience and what part of your brand story resonates with them.

6. Keep it concise.

Step 4: Build a Stellar Website

Your website is the heart of your brand. Build a personal website or contract a professional company to build it. Ensuring that your website is visually appealing, easy to navigate, and contains all the essential information about your expertise, services, and contact details is one of the ways to start building your brand.

What your website will need:

1. Clarify the goals of your website.
2. Have it designed with your brand look and feel.
3. Make sure it's a user-friendly design.
4. Align your website's design with your visual identity.
5. Craft engaging, informative content that communicates your expertise and resonates with your target audience.
6. Mobile-friendly design.
7. Create an About Me page.
8. Create a Services/Portfolio page.
9. Create a Blog or Content page.
10. Create a clear call-to-action (CTA).

* Retna Media has the expertise to build a stunning, user-friendly website that embodies your brand identity.

Step 5: Establish a Consistent Visual Identity

Consistency is vital to successful branding. Develop a visual identity that aligns with your brand story. Select a color palette, fonts, and a logo that reflects your personality and resonates with your target audience. Maintaining a consistent visual identity across all platforms creates a solid and memorable brand presence.

Steps to Establish Your Visual Identity

- **Logo Creation**
  Your logo is the cornerstone of your visual identity. Create a logo that represents your brand's DNA. It should be simple, memorable, and versatile enough to work across various platforms.

- **Color Palette**
  Choose colors that resonate with the brand's personality and values. Your color palette should be consistent across all branding materials, from your website to social media posts.

- **Typography Selection**
  Select fonts that align with your brand's tone and message. Use a combination of fonts—one for headings and another for body text—to maintain readability and visual interest.

And by all means, be consistent.

Step 6: The Power of Content Marketing

Content marketing is a potent tool to demonstrate your expertise and build a loyal following. Utilize blogs, videos, infographics, and social media platforms to share valuable insights and solutions for your audience. Engage with your audience regularly, respond to their comments, and participate in meaningful conversations.

Content marketing involves creating and distributing relevant, valuable, consistent content to attract and engage a target audience. This content should solve a problem with your audience. It can take various forms, such as blog posts, videos, infographics, podcasts, webinars, and more. The goal is to provide information that addresses your audience's pain points, educates them, and builds trust.

Why Content Marketing Matters

- Builds audience trust
- Search engine visibility
- Brand differentiation
- Long-term impact
- Builds a community of engaged followers

When you consistently deliver valuable content that resonates with your audience's needs, you're not just offering information; you're offering a valuable experience that solidifies your brand's position as a trusted and reliable source.

Step 7: Be Social on Social Media

Social media platforms are your brand's megaphone to the world. Choose the platforms that align with your target audience and establish a robust online presence. Post content consistently, interact with your followers, and collaborate with influencers in your niche. Social media will become your playground to engage, educate, and inspire.

Create a social media strategy and content calendar to help you and your team deliver strategic and exciting information for your audience.

Being social on social media is about building an active and engaged community around your brand. When you interact genuinely, offer value consistently, and create a positive online presence, you strengthen your brand's impact and create a virtual space where your audience feels connected, inspired, and valued.

Step 8: Analyze, Adapt, and Elevate

Measure the impact of your branding efforts through analytics. Analyze website traffic, social media metrics, and engagement levels. Use the insights gained to adapt your strategy continuously, refining your brand messaging and content to elevate your brand's impact and reach.

Imagine your brand as a living organism constantly evolving and growing. The final step in building your brand is a continuous analysis, adaptation, and elevation process. This step empowers you to refine your strategies, make data-driven decisions, and ensure your brand's impact increases.

Understanding Analysis, Adaptation, and Elevation

Building a personal brand is not a one-time effort. It's an ongoing journey that requires you to stay attuned to your audience's needs, industry trends, and the effectiveness of your strategies. By analyzing data, adapting to changes, and elevating your brand's presence, you ensure that your brand remains relevant and impactful.

Steps to Analyze, Adapt, and Elevate

- **Data Gathering**

  Collect and analyze data from various sources. This includes website analytics, social media metrics, engagement rates, and audience feedback.

- **Performance Assessment**

  Evaluate the performance of your content, campaigns, and overall brand strategy. Identify what's working well and what needs improvement.

- **Audience Insights**

  Gain deeper insights into your audience's preferences, behaviors, and pain points. Use surveys, polls, and direct feedback to understand them better.

Analyzing, adapting, and elevating your brand is a commitment to constant improvement. It's a recognition that the journey doesn't end after building your brand. It's a process of continual refinement that keeps your brand fresh, relevant, and impactful in a fast-changing world.

Time to Wrap it Up!

As we wrap up this journey of building a powerful personal brand, remember that you are not just creating a brand; you are crafting an identity that resonates, inspires, and leaves a lasting impact. Your brand is your unique story, expertise, and values combined into a compelling package that captures the hearts and minds of your audience.

Throughout this guide, we've navigated the intricate steps of building a personal brand, from uncovering your unique value proposition to leveraging social media. Each step is a building block, contributing to the solid foundation of your brand.

But the journey doesn't end here; it's a continuous evolution, an ongoing commitment to growth and refinement.

By embracing the power of personal branding, you're participating in a transformational process that can elevate your career, leverage, influence, and impact. Your brand has the potential to create ripples that extend beyond your immediate reach, inspiring others and leaving an indelible mark on your industry.

I'm more than just an expert; I'm your partner in your brand's journey. I'm committed to providing the tools, insights, and expertise you need to unlock your brand's potential. From designing a stunning website that reflects your identity to developing content that resonates with your audience, we're here to support you every step of the way.

Building a personal brand is not just about the destination; it's about the journey of discovering your uniqueness, connecting with your audience, and continually refining your presence. It's a journey that requires dedication, authenticity, and a willingness to evolve.

So, the next time you encounter a customer's choice that goes beyond reason, remember: "We don't buy products. We buy brands!" Let me be your guiding light in crafting a brand that captivates, connects, and conquers. Because a brand isn't just a product; it's a legacy in the making.

Download worksheets at www.retnamedia.com/brand-me

ABOUT THE AUTHOR

Fritz Colinet is a seasoned executive creative director and brand builder with over 25 years of expertise in marketing, brand development, and creative direction. With a lifelong passion for art and design, he pursued communications and design at Pratt in New York, establishing himself as an industry leader.

As the creative mind behind rebranding major brands such as Lady Foot Locker, The Houston Open, The Astorian, FullyRaw Kristina, and the Houston Dynamo, Fritz has demonstrated exceptional skills in revitalizing and modernizing iconic brands. His impressive portfolio led him to establish his own full-service branding and marketing agency, Retna Media, based in Houston.

Since its founding in 2005, Retna Media has successfully built and managed the brands of blue-chip companies and small businesses across diverse industries. Distinguished by strategic communication principles, the agency offers full-service offline and online marketing solutions powered by strategy, online marketing, and traditional advertising campaigns.

Fritz's dedication to fostering a corporate culture of "whatever it takes" ensures clients benefit from Retna Media's dedicated and intelligent processes. He also leads pro-bono campaigns that give back to the community and highlight corporate social responsibility.

Looking to the future, Fritz is committed to developing strategies for the globalization of brands and integrating technology-based solutions to support his clients' goals. His ultimate ambition is to establish Retna Media as the go-to advertising agency for brand marketing, pursuing this goal with passion, expertise, and unwavering dedication.

Own Your Thoughts; Own Your Results

Rick Loek

Let's get lost in thoughts and their influence on success and abundance. As we explore this topic, remember that "thoughts are things" holds a powerful truth that has been echoed in various forms throughout history. The concept resonates deeply from Napoleon Hill's *Think and Grow Rich* to Ernest Holmes's *The Science of Mind*.

THE SEED OF POSSIBILITY

Picture this: A humble garage cluttered with prototypes and dreams. Two friends, Steve Jobs and Steve Wozniak, ignited by an audacious thought: What if they could bring computing power to everyday people? Little did they know, this simple thought would blossom into Apple Inc., reshaping industries and defining an era.

In business, thoughts are more than fleeting notions; they are the seeds of possibility. Like Jobs and Wozniak, countless entrepreneurs have harnessed the power of their thoughts to transcend limitations and carve their path to success. But have you ever stopped to truly consider your thoughts' role in your business journey?

Have you ever considered the role your thoughts play in your business success? In a reality where thoughts are often dismissed as intangible whispers, it's time to embrace the truth: Thoughts are tangible forces that shape our perceptions, decisions, and outcomes. From the moment an idea takes root in your mind, it begins to manifest as reality.

Imagine the immense potential that lies within your thoughts. Just as a single seed can give rise to a towering oak, your thoughts can germinate into groundbreaking strategies, innovative products, and transformative solutions. But to realize this potential, you must recognize your thoughts' pivotal role in your business endeavors.

Throughout this chapter, we'll journey into the realm where the seeds of possibility are sown—your mind. Drawing inspiration from the timeless wisdom of *Think and Grow Rich* and the profound insights of *The Science of Mind*, we'll explore how thoughts serve as the catalysts for growth, how they shape your perception of what's achievable, and how they drive your actions in the business arena. By the end of this exploration, you'll be armed with the knowledge and tools to harness the power of your thoughts for unparalleled success.

As we venture further, consider this: If your thoughts were the blueprint for your business, what kind of foundation would you be laying? The journey of discovery begins now as we unveil the intricate connection between your thoughts and your journey toward prosperity. Are you ready to unlock the potential within your mind and embark on a transformative path of growth and abundance?

SHAPING YOUR REALITY THROUGH THOUGHTS

In the vast landscape of business, our thoughts act as sculptors, molding the contours of our reality. Just as an artist envisions a masterpiece before the first brushstroke, entrepreneurs conceptualize their ventures through the power of thought. Let's unveil the profound truth that our thoughts are the architects of what we perceive as possible.

EXPLORING THE PERCEPTION-SHAPING POWER OF THOUGHTS

Our thoughts serve as lenses through which we view the world. Consider this: When you encounter a challenge, do you see it as an insurmountable obstacle or a steppingstone to growth? Your thoughts shape this perception. *Think and Grow Rich* emphasizes the importance of cultivating a positive mental attitude, as it influences your ability to recognize opportunities even in adversity. By training your mind to perceive possibilities where others see roadblocks, you open doors to innovative solutions and uncharted territories.

CONFRONTING THE LIMITING BELIEFS PHENOMENON

Unfortunately, the terrain of entrepreneurship isn't immune to the presence of limiting beliefs. These beliefs, often rooted in past experiences or societal norms, create invisible barriers that hinder progress. *The Science of Mind* reminds us that our thoughts can set or dissolve limits. When entrepreneurs believe they cannot achieve a goal, their thoughts become self-fulfilling prophecies. Overcoming this phenomenon requires introspection and a willingness to challenge assumptions. By acknowledging and reframing these beliefs, entrepreneurs can break free from their confines and reach new heights of success.

ILLUSTRATING THE IMPACT

❊ Imagine two aspiring business owners with the same opportunity—to develop a groundbreaking app in a booming market. One, let's call her Sarah, is fueled by thoughts of innovation and growth. She envisions her app transforming the way people engage with technology. The other, Mark, is plagued by doubts and fears. He dwells on potential setbacks and worries about competition. While Sarah seizes the opportunity, Mark hesitates, eventually letting the chance slip through his fingers.

Sarah's optimistic thoughts propelled her to embrace the opportunity, while Mark's limiting beliefs held him back. Their outcomes were shaped by external factors and the thoughts that guided their choices.

We've journeyed into perception and its intricate connection to thoughts. From perceiving challenges as growth opportunities to dismantling limiting beliefs, your thoughts wield the power to shape your reality. Remember that the lens through which you view the world is uniquely yours. By cultivating a thought process that fosters abundance and growth, you can navigate the business landscape confidently and resiliently, transcending the confines of perceived limitations.

FROM MINDSET TO ACTION:
THE THOUGHT-BEHAVIOR CONNECTION

In the intricate dance of business, our thoughts shape our perceptions and guide our actions. Consider this: Every decision you make, every strategy you implement, and every step you take is a manifestation of your thoughts. We will now delve into the profound interplay between thoughts and behavior, uncovering how the two are intricately connected.

THE INFLUENCE OF THOUGHTS ON ACTIONS AND DECISIONS

Our thoughts are the silent architects of our behaviors. *Think and Grow Rich* highlights the critical role of definiteness of purpose—aligning your thoughts with clear goals. This alignment becomes the driving force behind your actions. If you envision expanding your market reach, your thoughts will guide you to make decisions that align with this vision, leading to the pursuit of new opportunities and partnerships.

THE NEUROLOGICAL UNDERPINNINGS

THE RETICULAR ACTIVATING SYSTEM

The connection between thoughts and behavior is deeply rooted in the neurological realm. Our brain's reticular activating system (RAS) acts as a gatekeeper, filtering the vast sea of information to focus on what aligns with our thoughts and goals. When you set your mind on a specific outcome, your RAS attests to opportunities and information relevant to that goal.

❋ SHIFTING FROM THOUGHT TO TANGIBLE CHANGE

Let's meet Lisa, a small business owner struggling to stand out in a competitive market. She's been toiling tirelessly, yet her efforts seem futile. One day, she stumbles upon the concept that her thoughts can shape her reality. She realizes that her constant worry about failure affects her decisions and actions.

Lisa decides to shift her thought process. She embraces a positive mindset and envisions her business flourishing. With this shift, she begins to explore new marketing strategies and innovative product ideas. She joins networking events and collaborates with like-minded entrepreneurs. As her actions align with her newfound positive thoughts, she starts seeing tangible changes. Her revenue starts climbing.

As you reflect on your journey, consider how your thoughts guide your decisions and actions. By nurturing a mindset that aligns with your goals and values, you can harness the innate potential to shape your business strategies and drive tangible, transformative change.

CULTIVATING A PROSPERITY MINDSET

The seeds of success are sown in strategies, actions, and the soil of your mindset. Enter the "prosperity mindset," a transformative approach that fosters abundance, growth, and resilience. It's time to explore how this mindset can become the cornerstone of your business journey, driving you to heights you never thought possible.

EMBRACING THE PROSPERITY MINDSET

At its core, the prosperity mindset is an orientation toward abundance. It's the belief that opportunities are abundant, challenges are steppingstones, and success is attainable through dedicated effort and continuous learning. This concept aligns closely with the groundbreaking research of psychologist Carol Dweck, who introduced the concept of a fixed versus growth mindset. While a fixed mindset traps individuals in the belief that their abilities are static, a growth mindset empowers them to embrace challenges as opportunities for development.

The Wisdom of Carol Dweck's Research

Carol Dweck's work holds a mirror to our beliefs about our potential. Imagine a business owner, Maria, who faces a setback in her product launch. A fixed mindset might lead her to believe that this failure defines her capabilities, causing her to shy away from future endeavors. In contrast, a growth mindset enables Maria to view the setback as a learning experience. She identifies areas for improvement, adapts her strategy, and emerges stronger.

Nurturing a Prosperity Mindset

Practical Tips: Cultivating a prosperity mindset requires intentional effort and practice. The following are practical tips to help you foster this mindset and infuse it into your business journey.

1. **Positive Self-Talk:** Monitor your self-talk and replace self-limiting phrases with affirmations that reinforce your potential.

2. **Continuous Learning:** Embrace a thirst for knowledge and see every challenge as an opportunity to learn and improve.

3. **Embrace Failure:** Shift your perspective on failure from defeat to valuable feedback. Use it to refine your strategies and decisions.

4. **Goal Setting:** Set ambitious yet achievable goals that encourage growth and push you beyond your comfort zone.

5. **Surrounding Yourself:** Surround yourself with positive, growth-oriented individuals who uplift and inspire you.

6. **Mindfulness and Visualization:** Practice mindfulness and visualize your success, reinforcing the belief that your goals are attainable.

By adopting a prosperity mindset, you're fostering a foundation of optimism, resilience, and abundance. With each thought and action aligned with this mindset, you create a harmonious ecosystem for your business to flourish.

Your thoughts are the architects of your mindset, and your mindset is the compass that guides your journey. By embracing the philosophy of abundance and growth, you're not just changing your business but your entire approach to success.

OVERCOMING CHALLENGES WITH THOUGHT RESILIENCE

Challenges in the dynamic business landscape are not mere outliers but integral to the journey. However, it's not the challenges that define your trajectory but how you respond to them. Enter the art of thought resilience—the ability to navigate obstacles with a mindset that turns setbacks into springboards for growth.

NAVIGATING CHALLENGES

The Influence of Thoughts: Challenges are the litmus tests of your business acumen and adaptability. In the face of adversity, your thoughts play a pivotal role in determining whether you succumb to or rise above setbacks. *Think and Grow Rich* emphasizes the importance of maintaining a positive attitude even when faced with challenges, as thoughts can shape your response and subsequent actions.

THE POWER OF COGNITIVE REFRAMING

Cognitive reframing, a psychological technique, allows you to shift your perspective on challenges. Changing how you interpret a situation can alter your emotional response and, subsequently, your actions. This technique aligns seamlessly with the teachings of *The Science of Mind*, which highlights the malleability of thoughts and their role in reshaping reality.

CASE STUDY: TURNING SETBACKS INTO STEPPINGSTONES

❉ Consider the story of Alex, a visionary entrepreneur who faced a substantial supply chain disruption. Initially, he was overwhelmed by frustration and stress, fearing the potential impact on his business's reputation. However, Alex recognized the power of his thoughts in shaping his response. He embraced cognitive reframing, viewing the disruption as an opportunity to explore alternative suppliers and streamline operations.

His actions followed suit as Alex shifted his thoughts from despair to resilience. He collaborated with his team to identify innovative solutions, negotiated with new suppliers, and implemented backup plans. The disruption became a turning point. Alex resolved the crisis, and his business emerged more robust and adaptable than before.

Alex's journey underscores the transformative potential of thought resilience. By fostering a mindset that sees challenges as opportunities for growth, you can empower yourself to face adversity head-on and emerge stronger on the other side.

In conclusion, thought resilience is not merely about bouncing back from challenges; it's about using your thoughts to bounce forward. As you navigate the tumultuous waters of business, remember that the lens through which you view challenges shapes your reality. By mastering the art of thought resilience, you're not just confronting difficulties but using them as steppingstones toward a brighter, more prosperous future.

COLLABORATION AND COMMUNICATION

THE ROLE OF THOUGHTS IN RELATIONSHIPS

In the intricate tapestry of business, relationships are the threads that weave success together. But have you considered how the very thoughts that inhabit your mind influence the dynamics of collaboration and communication? In this section, we delve into the profound role of thought in shaping relationships, fostering empathy, and driving effective collaboration.

THE SILENT LANGUAGE OF THOUGHTS IN COMMUNICATION

Communication in business isn't just about words; it's a delicate dance of thoughts exchanged between individuals. Consider a scenario where differing viewpoints arise during a team meeting. The thoughts you hold regarding your colleagues' perspectives shape your response. You'll likely engage in a productive dialogue if you approach these thoughts openly and curiously. On the other hand, if you cling to preconceived notions, communication can become a barrier rather than a bridge.

EMPATHETIC LISTENING: BRIDGING THOUGHT AND UNDERSTANDING

Empathy—the ability to understand and share the feelings of another—hinges on the thoughts you cultivate during conversations. *The Science of Mind* underlines the power of thought in fostering empathy, enabling you to step into someone else's shoes and see the world through their lens. You create a space for authentic connection and deeper understanding by quieting your thoughts and genuinely listening.

SCENARIO: UNLEASHING THE POWER OF OPEN-MINDED EXCHANGE

❊ Imagine a group of diverse entrepreneurs tasked with developing a collaborative project. Each participant brings their unique set of experiences and thoughts to the table. One entrepreneur, Maria, advocates for a traditional approach, while another, Malik, suggests an innovative method. Instead of dismissing each other's thoughts, they engage in an open-minded discussion.

Through empathetic listening, Maria understands Malik's perspective is rooted in a desire to innovate, not disregarding tradition. Malik, in turn, appreciates Maria's respect for proven methodologies. This exchange of thoughts leads to a synergy of ideas, where Maria and Malik combine tradition with innovation to create a groundbreaking solution. Their collaboration thrives not despite their differing thoughts but because of them.

In essence, collaboration and communication are vehicles driven by the thoughts we bring to the table. By embracing open-mindedness and empathetic listening, you're not just engaging in dialogue but fostering connections that transcend individual perspectives.

As we conclude this chapter, remember that the thoughts you harbor shape your business strategies and the relationships that nurture your journey. By honing your thought processes to embody empathy, openness, and collaboration, you're enhancing your business acumen and creating a foundation for a thriving network of interconnected success.

Summary

Harnessing the Thought Advantage

As we end this enlightening journey through the realm of thoughts and their profound impact on business success, let's reflect on the key insights that have emerged.

Shaping Your Reality

Our thoughts are more than fleeting notions; they are potent architects of our perception and reality. By adopting a positive mindset that sees challenges as opportunities and potential as boundless, you can open doors to innovation and transformation.

From Mindset to Action

The connection between thoughts and actions is undeniable. Every decision, every strategy, and every step you take is rooted in the fertile soil of your thoughts. By aligning your thoughts with your goals and leveraging the neurological power of cognitive reframing, you can navigate the business landscape with purpose and determination.

Cultivating a Prosperity Mindset

The prosperity mindset is the compass that steers your journey. Through the wisdom of Carol Dweck's research, we've learned that a growth-oriented perspective enhances problem-solving and fuels your potential for growth. You nurture optimism, resilience, and abundance by embracing a prosperity mindset.

Overcoming Challenges with Thought Resilience

Challenges are inevitable in business, but your response to them defines your path. Thought resilience empowers you to transform setbacks into steppingstones for growth. You can turn adversity into innovation by nurturing a mindset that embraces obstacles as opportunities.

Collaboration and Communication

Relationships are at the heart of business, and the thoughts you bring to them shape their dynamics. Empathetic listening and open-minded exchange are the cornerstones of effective collaboration. You're building a network of interconnected success by fostering connections that transcend individual perspectives.

Reiterating the Central Message

This chapter has echoed a central message: Your thoughts are the foundation of what you perceive as achievable. Every thought you harbor, every belief you hold, shapes the reality you inhabit. Your mindset isn't just a passive observer but a powerful force driving your journey.

Take Action

As you embark on your business endeavors, remember that the power to achieve greatness resides within your mind. By harnessing the potential of your thoughts, you're not just embracing success; you're becoming the architect of your destiny. So, dare to dream boldly, think expansively, and let your thoughts be the guiding stars that lead you to unparalleled business success.

In the symphony of life and business, your thoughts are the melody that shapes the grand composition of your journey. With each note, each belief, and each intention, you're sculpting a masterpiece that reflects your unique vision and potential. Embrace the thought advantage, and may your path be illuminated by the brilliance of your thoughts.

For a deeper understanding and further reading, please see http://TheAmazingRick.com.

1. Napoleon Hill. (1937). Think and Grow Rich. New York: Ralston Society.
2. Ernest Holmes. (1926). The Science of Mind. Los Angeles: Jeremy P. Tarcher/Penguin.
3. Dweck, C. S. (2006). Mindset: The New Psychology of Success. Random House.

ABOUT THE AUTHOR

The Amazing Rick is a trailblazing visionary with a penchant for business transformation and personal growth. Rick is a master of multiple domains and a catalyst for empowerment and upliftment.

Rick founded and operates three enterprises:

1. Onesta Wealth Management, LLC is a registered investment advisor company that navigates the complex landscape of retirement planning.
2. Calrima Senior Services and Insurance Solutions is an insurance brokerage specializing in various insurance products.
3. Little Grass Shack Coaching is a coaching company that bears the promise of its name—a sanctuary where success blooms. With a specialized focus on success

coaching, he empowers individuals, companies, and groups to unearth their latent potential, fostering a culture of growth and upliftment.

However, it's not just expertise that sets Rick apart; it's his mastery of neuro-linguistic programming (NLP), hypnosis, and mental and emotional release (MER). As a trainer and master practitioner, he has unlocked the potential of these transformative modalities, shaping lives and destinies in the process.

Rick invites you to join him on a journey of transformation, where the ordinary transforms into the extraordinary, and every challenge becomes an opportunity to thrive.

How to Scale & Grow Your Business: The Sales Perspective

Amy Lau

This is your time and opportunity.

Tools like AI assist in leveling the playing field by lowering the barriers to entry in scaling your business. While more prominent corporations struggle to stay relevant, small businesses are agile enough to leverage new technologies to personalize offerings, build relationships, and gain clientele.

Have you ever watched a three-legged race? It's a fun game that tests coordination, teamwork, and mutual understanding between partners. While amusing at picnics, it offers profound lessons for business. Scaling a company requires alignment, collaboration, and synergy across departments—just like runners racing with their legs tied.[1]

Let's talk about your three-legged scenario in growing and scaling your business and sales.

1. **Innovation** (product engineering/operations/execution) is vision and building solutions. But alone, without sales and financial prudence, even the best ideas remain just that.

2. **Sales** gives innovations market value. Salespeople need excellent products, positioning, and systems to succeed. They spend time building relationships, positioning solutions, and creating customers. But without operational support and profitable finances, the impact diminishes. It's critical that all systems and personnel, regardless of title or role, are aligned and focused on enabling the sales transactions of products from inception to delivery.

3. **Financial Management Strategy** ensures profitability and sustainable growth. With competing pressures of risk mitigation and enabling investments, financial leaders balance short- and long-term views. This requires coordination across departments to enable sales and sustain the business cycle.

Traditionally, in business, two foundational "legs" are innovation and financial management strategy. Innovation entails innovating products and managing operations to execution. Financial Strategy involves financial planning to ensure

---

[1]   Bennett, B., & Bennett, M. (2004). The Complete Idiot's Guide to Team-Building. Alpha.

profitability and sustainability. But without the third leg—Sales—even the best innovations amount to just a hobby. Sales is the lifeblood of any organization, monetizing innovations to customers.

For companies to scale, these legs must move in unison, like championship racers. If innovation outpaces demand, companies trip on unchecked growth. If sales race ahead of product readiness and support systems, reputation suffers. And without profitability, companies collapse before taking flight. Successful businesses understand this delicate balance; their teams respect each aspect's importance while working diligently toward synchronization. Their reward isn't only success in their endeavor, but also knowing that their balanced method is key to their competitive standing.

When aligned, these three legs enable businesses to thrive. But without communication and a shared vision, growth is painful. Like runners stumbling over mismatched steps, misaligned teams trip up progress. Still, these struggles can be overcome with resilience and commitment to collaboration.

The following case studies are stories of clients whose names were changed to protect their privacy. Perhaps you can learn from their challenges in creating your big dream—a bountiful, rewarding, scalable business that feeds your passion—so you can leave a legacy you can be proud of.

Business Case #1 – ABC Corporation

Stewart had a big dream to be a successful business owner. Like many entrepreneurs, he was tired of working his nine-to-five grind and dreamed of using his top-notch technical skills to own his own business.

After an important client said they'd hire him if he went independent, Stewart quit his job, set up a SaaS revenue model, and hired Neal to succeed him so he could spend time with family. He also hired some local techies to serve clients.

Simultaneously, Stewart initiated a Hong Kong branch.

Despite a promising start, several hurdles emerged:

1. **No marketing Plan:** Stewart's passion was evident, but he had no formal business training or mentor. He crafted a business plan but not a marketing plan that defined his niche and competition. Lacking a clear vision and strategy, his venture diverged from his dreams.

2. **Overexpansion:** Stewart simultaneously juggled the start-up, grooming Neal, and initiating the Hong Kong branch, overextending himself. His frequent travels abroad strained things at home and work.

3. **The trap of Indispensability:** Stewart's absence paralyzed operations, hurting family time. He felt indispensable, priding himself on being needed, delaying breaks until things smoothed out. His business was running him, not vice versa.

4. **Inefficient systems and processes:**

   - A CRM was acquired to keep track of sales, but no processes were put in place to support sales and order fulfillment.

   - There were no defined sales processes, avatars, client journey maps, presentations, tracking, or reporting to support the sales effort.

   - The unclear pricing model left clients perplexed. Every lead necessitated a customized and tailored proposal. Costs weren't itemized, complicating alterations and dragging negotiations.

5. **No pricing strategy:**

   - Stewart's initial promotion grandfathered pricing for early adopters because he wanted testimonials, which lacked foresight for profitability.
   - Subsequent clients faced a complex pricing questionnaire. Lengthy negotiations often followed, which prompted losing clients to competitive bids.

6. **Sales was an afterthought:** Neither Stewart nor Neal had sales knowledge. Neal winged it initially alongside operations. They eventually hired Julie, but lacked pricing clarity to train her team on proposals. While Julie was onboarding, she simultaneously trained Neal and the sales team (a free, borrowed resource from Stewart's client) on cold calling to set appointments. After three months of training a team that produced lackluster results, that client recalled his team for other projects, leaving Stewart with no resources for Julie to work with.

7. **No financial oversight:** Stewart managed finances alone to save costs. But this overlooked revenue optimization, impacting profits and team workload.

Stewart prioritized technology and clients, not sales and finances. Neal was operations focused, not leadership material. Stewart hired engineers with familiar proficiencies, not those with diverse skills. Moreover, roles were mismatched. Neal, an operational stalwart, wasn't leadership material but a mere yes-man.

As a result, Stewart's wife paid the bills amidst revenue shortfalls. Stewart ran a hobby, not a viable business. Absent were a clear vision, a sequentially structured plan, and a defined strategy with measurable milestones. Sales were an afterthought, complicating profitability and preventing him from taking the business to the next level.

Key Takeaways:

1. **Financial management strategy**

   - **Hire those with diverse expertise,** not people just like yourself. Stewart's technical acumen, while a strength, needed complementing with diversified talent in other divisions. Relying solely on his expertise without integrating a broader range of skills held back growth.

   - **Take time off.** Are you working *on* your business or *in* it? Be able to take time off for your well-being. Focus on productivity and results, not just being busy.

   - **Financial oversight:** Overlooking the necessity of adequate financial governance can lead to a lopsided pricing strategy and revenue losses.

2. **Sales**

   - **Lead with sales as a priority, not an afterthought.** Don't bottleneck sales, the lifeblood of your business. Equip your salespeople with the tools to succeed because *their* success is *your* success. A profitable organization needs robust sales processes and trained personnel. ABC's ad-hoc approach led to inefficiencies, complicating client conversions.

3. **Innovation**

   - **Scale by establishing protocols (standard operating procedures) for decision-making while you are away.** Empower your team to follow your vision.

The key to scaling a business is your ability to translate your passion into delivering value and driving results—with sales being the bridge between you and your customers. How do you navigate that bridge? Start with a business plan and a marketing plan that includes your SWOT (strengths, weaknesses, opportunities, and threats) analysis to identify who your niche audience is, any pain points or challenges they're undergoing, and which needs or gaps your business can fulfill. This allows you to ground your passion in real market opportunities.

Stewart's venture underscores the need for a balanced tripod of Sales, Innovation, and Financial Management Strategy. Absence or weakness in all three legs has destabilized his organization, stunting its potential and growth.

Business Case #2 – Old School Corporation (OSC)

Meet Tom, a business owner who's been running OSC, a SaaS services company, for over a decade. Tom has an engineering and technical mind, and he hired CFO (Phil) and COO (George), trusted cronies he previously worked with. OSC had an advisory board and established marketing and sales systems. Sales were mainly derived from word of mouth. because they had a reputation for providing quality at a fraction of the cost. Once a year, the Head of Marketing and the CEO attended the Computer and Electronics Conference in Las Vegas, where they were sure to get a few more customers to buy their services.

Some challenges in Tom's business:

1. **Stagnant growth mindset:** Tom engaged with a business coach early on, only to disengage six months later, choosing to focus on increasing sales over building

his foundational mindset. His half-hearted engagement and eventual reluctance to continue showcased a complacency and overconfidence that hampered the evolution of his leadership.

2. **A patriarchal culture** that failed to encourage open communication: His CFO (Phil) and COO (George) were both yes-men whose skills were limited to primarily following orders. Furthermore, Tom ran a tight ship, and everything—even the slightest decisions— had to pass through him. He had a hard time letting go of the reins.

3. **Hierarchical culture undermines loyalty:** Phil and George, reflecting Tom's patriarchal leadership, mirrored a similar hierarchical and nondiverse organizational setup. Hiring people within their comfort zone created an echo chamber that lacked creativity. This unspoken mandate of hiring "controllable" talent led to a cascade of trust issues, further constricting the free flow of ideas. This led to:

   - **Underutilization of talent:** Having Phil in a nominal CFO role was a disservice. Tom failed to leverage Phil's potential strategic insights by reducing him to a glorified bookkeeper.

   - **Gender bias:** The women at OSC faced a double jeopardy. With limited decision-making powers, they were relegated to secondary roles, even though their titles didn't reflect such. This hurt the company's diversity and created a gendered inefficiency that stifled creativity and innovation.

   - **Rampant nepotism:** Tom hired his son, Johnny, who had just graduated with a liberal arts degree, to work for and be trained by Arlene, the head of marketing. The assurance of job security for one was a costly trade-off that compromised morale for many. Johnny visibly fell asleep on camera during Zoom calls with the team, yet no one called him out. As witnessed by Arlene's resignation after three months of training Johnny, employee morale deteriorated.

- **Innovation drought:** Employees operated out of fear rather than passion. This environment, though it ensured obedience, suffocated innovation. Loyal yet unempowered employees hindered rather than helped the company's growth trajectory.

4. **Financial conservatism:** Tom's reluctance to spend in the business, albeit commendable in his personal life, stunted business growth. His fiscal conservancy meant that the company lacked agility and proactiveness.

- **Competitive disadvantage:** The lack of benefits at OSC, although culturally acceptable, meant that OSC constantly bled talent, unable to compete.
- **High turnover:** A revolving door of employees resulted in operational inefficiencies and the loss of intellectual capital. This cycle of hire-train-lose-rehire meant Tom was fighting fires versus steering the ship forward.

5. **Sales struggles:**

- **Misaligned talent acquisition:** While initially making strides with sales expert Katrina, Tom's attempt to save on sales compensation led him to hire Joe, a novice salesperson with undeveloped sales skills, a mismatch for the complex sales role that required building relationships and negotiating with the C-suite. Joe's inefficiencies and hesitations diluted the company's ability to close business.

- **Customer attrition:** High turnover and inconsistent support upset OSC's longtime customers. Disjointed handover processes and prolonged training times for internal support replacements eroded client trust and confidence, rendering client retention difficult.

Key Takeaways:

1. **Sales**

   - **Prioritize sales, customer acquisition, and retention:** A successful business must have a competent sales force and prioritize customer acquisition and retention. OSC's missteps in sales hires and inconsistent customer support exemplified this.

2. **Financial Management**

   - **HR Problems: High turnover, nepotism, gender bias, and outdated culture/hiring/onboarding practices** led to attrition and compromised employee morale. Without proper onboarding, employee success was a guessing game. Not only was it costly to rehire and train new employees, but customer retention became an issue as their brand reputation was tarnished.

   - **Overly conservative financial management:** Conservative spending can be an asset, but not when it blinds a business to market realities. With no real CFO influence and an aversion to offering competitive employee benefits, OSC missed opportunities for sustainable growth.

3. **Innovation**
   - With its patriarchal hierarchy, OSC missed the opportunity to fully blossom and innovate. A lack of diversification in thought and talent, combined with financial rigidity, left the company continually catching up rather than leading the way.

The lesson: While individual strengths are essential, a business thrives on collaboration, adaptability, and a harmonized approach across sales, innovation, and financial management.

For all its missteps, OSC could be turned around. Give the executive team autonomy to make decisions. Encourage communications across departments. Clear communication between Sales and Support could nip a customer problem in the bud. Proper benefits and compensation could boost morale, foster loyalty, and retain employees' knowledge, cutting training costs.

BUSINESS CASE #3 – ZENITH CORPORATION

At the helm of Zenith, Rachel, a seasoned CEO, fostered an environment characterized by collaboration, agility, and vision. Adeptly leading a competent management team comprising Jim (CFO), Edgar (CTO), and Francis (Head of Sales), Zenith's triumphs were no accident.

Zenith, specializing in tax advisory services, was a paragon of operational excellence. They had robust systems to manage and support sales, and their sales team also showcased versatility and insight. This synergy between tools and talent, bolstered by strategic compensation and incentives, created a high-performance cycle.

When a unique, time-sensitive sales opportunity emerged, Zenith didn't buckle under pressure. They assessed, strategized, and executed a quick pivot to create a new product. This steadfast entrepreneurial mindset of product innovation differentiates them from the competition. They introduced the Channel Partner Program to sell this solution, adding agility to its already impressive speed. By offering partners compensation incentives and even unprecedented access to Zenith's internal sales support team, Zenith expanded its reach and strengthened its network. This strategic move and underlying trust ethos culminated in record-breaking sales for Zenith.

Key Takeaways:

1. **Sales**
   - **Sales excellence:** Zenith had a well-oiled sales machine that was versatile, competent, and empowered. Their seamless CRM process, communication with Marketing, and strategic incentives showcased a robust sales structure. By valuing their extended team of Channel Partners, they quickly developed a stronghold in market share before competitors arrived.

2. **Financial Management**
   - **Sound financial spending focused on ROI:** Jim's financial acumen ensured Zenith's stability. Zenith demonstrated the importance of strategic financial planning in growth and scalability by incentivizing internal salespeople and external partners.

   - **Streamlined operations support innovation:** With Edgar as CTO, Zenith had integrated robust systems like CRM and ERP, critical for scalable business operations. Such infrastructure allows for agility, primarily when the need for rapid pivots arises.

3. **Innovation**
   - The executive team actively stays ahead of the curve, developing innovative products to diversify their portfolio.

Zenith exemplified synchronized success. Due to their collaborative spirit, agility, and robust systems, Zenith is poised for a desirable exit strategy, should they choose—be it a prosperous retirement for Rachel or selling the business for a lucrative profit.

Recap and Summary

The first case, ABC Corporation, depicted an organization struggling with sales strategies that didn't equate to productivity. Despite the efforts and activities, the core components of the business were out of alignment: no visionary leadership, standardized pricing structure, developed sales flow, or financial management.

The second case, Tom's Old School Corporation (OSC), had inefficiencies rooted in a patriarchal, centralized leadership that stifled innovation, creating bottlenecks across sales, customer support, and financial management. High turnover cost them valuable IP. Twenty-first-century business leadership calls for unwavering diversity of people, perspectives, and ideas—without which companies are left to flounder.

ABC and OSC are different manifestations of the old management styles of the twentieth century. This traditional egoic approach impedes business growth. However, both cases can be turned around—if they shift their mindsets and begin instituting the fundamentals described in this chapter.

In contrast to ABC and OSC, Zenith stood apart. We saw a well-oiled machine with integrated processes, a collaborative leadership approach, and a readiness to adapt. Trust and transparency were built into their relationships and partnerships across the board, leaving no room for failure. Zenith had solidified all three legs of the business (innovations, sales, and finance), resulting in a model of sustainable success.

CALL TO ACTION

Costly mistakes are preventable at the early stage. Set up your business on a solid structure to avoid unnecessary risks that could stump your organization and derail your growth. If you initially missed some of these steps, you can always correct course by assessing, reviewing, and restructuring to fortify your foundation. Restoring your **scalability** restores your **saleability**.

To all twenty-first-century business leaders aspiring to scale, the path is clear: Embrace all three legs of your business by ensuring sales, innovation, and financial management are synchronized, robust, and ready to adapt.

Use all the technology tools (i.e., AI) available to build strong relationships internally with your team and channel partners and externally with your customers.

To build strong relationships with customers, seek first to understand their needs. In the 1920s, while Ford's Model-T only came in one color (black), GM asked their customers what kind of car they wanted and then listened. While Model-Ts remained unchanged, GM added different colors and features yearly—more horsepower, brakes, sleeker designs, and shock absorption. GM offered installment plans and trade-in options to combat Model-T's affordable price. By 1927, GM's responsiveness gained them over one million new buyers, compared to Ford's 481,000. GM had "run Goliath off the road."[2]

Good relationships strengthen trust, which enables sales to happen, thus securing your company's ongoing success. Put differently, *building relationships is the only way businesses can move forward.* We need each other to thrive.

Your zenith awaits.

ABOUT THE AUTHOR

Amy Lau moved from Hong Kong to the US at eight years old, driven by her family's pursuit of a brighter future. Overcoming barriers as an immigrant, she mastered English to advocate and negotiate for her parents.

Attending the University of Washington laid the foundation for a successful career spanning two decades. She's worked with IBM, Oracle, Microsoft, Cisco, and Salesforce, exceeding $100 million in revenues and winning multiple prestigious awards.

Amy has a natural ability to establish profound connections and cultivate lasting relationships. She coaches business owners to achieve sales hypergrowth while navigating fast-paced, competitive landscapes.

Blending business administration and literary fiction degrees, Amy uses a values-based approach to build trust by sincerely understanding her clients' challenges and helping them reach their visions.

In business, Amy believes in empathy and unwavering commitment. Collaborating with her opens doors to a transformative

---

[2]   https://www.poconorecord.com/story/lifestyle/2006/05/21/
      may-25-1927-ford-s/50205874007/

journey of success, guided by her visionary leadership and profound connections. The path to enduring triumph in a dynamic business world becomes brilliantly clear with Amy by your side.

Together with her business partner and husband, they utilize a holistic, well-rounded approach to advise their clients in sales, finance, and operational strategies, including go-to-market, scaling, or exit.

Seek Golden Moments in Communication

Sheila Jones

Effective communication - no matter the purpose - requires intentionality. Throughout my life, I have worked to improve my communication effectiveness and achieved high-level communication abilities with application across diverse work forces and business industries.

Effective communication requires a "straightforward" exchange between a speaker and a listener.

As a college student, I majored in food science. It was mandatory to take a communication and public speaking class.

However, I was baffled as to where and how I would apply this skill after graduation.

As the semester started, our professor reviewed the syllabus. I learned that I was required to deliver three separate speeches, a three-, five-, and fifteen-minute speech - all with increasing complexity.

My three-minute speech was scheduled for February 14th. For this speech, I challenged myself to think differently and find something fun, engaging, and memorable. I chose to acknowledge, recognize, and celebrate Valentine's Day. On speech day, I began by engaging the intellectual side of the students with the historical timeline of Valentine's Day. I continued by sharing simple yet entertaining jokes. As I closed the speech, I gave each person a small bag of iconic chalk-like conversation hearts stamped with heartfelt messages like, "Be mine!" I remember asking my classmates, "How did I do?" The response was this: "You did great! You did great!" Honestly, I never knew what that meant. Did they understand the content? Did they get my jokes? Personally, I considered it a success because I did not faint.

The professor assigned the topics for the five - and fifteen - minute speeches. I do not recall the topics, the preparation, or the speeches. Maybe I was nervous, maybe the content was just so dull, or maybe I did not present the content in a way to create a lasting memory.

As I reflect on these speeches, there was a common theme: "straightforward", "fulfillment of time" and "word count." Being young in my communication journey, I had yet to develop a full set of communication skills. I did not understand that effective communication should be focused on the audience's comprehension.

Effective communication requires "measuring" the audience's comprehension.

Eventually, I graduated, and my professional career began. In 2010, I was recruited to join a big retailer. It was a different work environment. Most of my team members were business experts, while I was a scientist.

I was managing a high-profile project for the formulation improvement of our laundry detergent. Laundry detergent is a highly scientific and complex product with an emotional connection. The process is segmented into phases: Phase one is stains and fabric selection. The stain can be grass, mustard, red wine, while the fabric selection options range from cotton to polyester. The second phase is the equipment selection, which includes using consumer equivalent washing machines and dryers. The third phase identifies and implements testing attributes, such as percentage of stain removal and fragrance retention. The fourth and final stage is data collation and final performance reports.

The laundry industry and consumers measure performance by the percentage of stain removal and fragrance retention. The consumer is highly offended if either metric fails to meet expectations.

As I worked on the project, I gave weekly status updates. Over time, we reached the formulation approval time window. As I readied for the presentation, I collected my stain swatches and fabric samples and studied the extensive performance reports. I was ready to share the standard deviation and the probability of customer liking score. I was confident we would approve the formulation improvement. The room was filled with decision-makers and decision-implementers. I talked for approximately twenty minutes, and when I finally stopped talking, I looked around the room, I was shocked to see blank stares, bored decision-makers, and disengaged team members scrolling on their phones. I stumbled to find the words to engage the group. The top merchant kindly and respectfully said, "We ran out of time and need to leave. You are going to need to reschedule."

I sought feedback from my coworker, who looked me straight in the eyes and said, "No one wants to hear about science; no one understands this testing. You lost them." Ouch! That was painful but honest feedback. Unfortunately, I wasted this team's time.

The brutal feedback forced me to dive deeper into my communication skills and look for ways to improve my effectiveness. I needed to stop talking and start delivering golden moments of communication.

For the second laundry detergent presentation, I opted to skip the complicated reports and graphs and focus on audience participation, engagement, and comprehension. I went to a local retailer and purchased two packs of white t-shirts, a Sharpie, and the food and beverage products notoriously dropped on our shirts.

To simplify the complex science, I created a stain guide. I prepared the shirts by drawing circles labeling the food and grass stains areas. I proceeded to place the food items in the circles on the shirts. I let the food items sit for five minutes which allowed a stain to develop in the fabric. Next, I chose the typical consumer stain removal method which included frantically rubbing the stain with a wet napkin. However, not all stains were fully removed. I then focused on the grass stains. I took a simple application approach. I literally rubbed the shirt in my grass. This provided an authentic green grass stain. I again mimicked the consumer removal method by brushing off the grass stain. Once again, there was partial removal.

We headed off to the local laundry mat with a roll of quarters. To determine the effectiveness of the stain removal and ultimately performance of the laundry detergent, we paired each soiled shirt with a test formulation of laundry detergent.

The washing and drying commenced, and eventually the shirts were put on coat hangers. They looked great! I sent a meeting notice inviting the team for round two of The Laundry Detergent Decision.

As we kicked off round two, I started the meeting by apologizing for the lack of success during our first meeting. I said, "Today, I will communicate our results differently. I would like you to first observe that we have multiple T-shirts hanging on hangers around the room. These shirts represent the actual performance of the laundry detergent when stained with typical food, beverage, and grass stains." I continued, "We will use a stain guide as a reference point to identify and compare a previously stained, unwashed shirt to a stained washed shirt." I explained to the team that excellent detergent will remove 100 percent of the stain and if there is a residual stain, the detergent underperformed. After a few minutes, the decision-makers and decision-implementers were fully engaged and evaluating the detergents' performance.

All around the room you could see them touching the shirts, studying the stains, comparing shirts and detergents. Additionally, they were smelling the shirts and calling out the fragrance. I overheard our top merchant say he was shocked to see how effective the removal of red wine was and disappointed to see grass stains after washing. We reached a very quick decision, and I received accolades for the presentation, and it was a golden communication moment.

Why did round one fail? It failed for two reasons: I was talking "straightforward" to my audience and sharing a message centered around my skill set, my scientific skill set. I did not consider "measuring" the team's comprehension during the presentation. Simply put, I was disconnected from my audience. I figured they understood what I was talking about.

Why was the Laundry Detergent Decision round two successful? I was focused on the audience. I took the complex science and made it simple to understand, increasing audience comprehension. When our merchants saw residual grass stains, it reminded them of their grass-stained pants. I also met them intellectually. They needed data but not my scientific standard deviation data. They needed data a merchant would understand. As each person grabbed a shirt, they became engaged participants, and I was actively "measuring" the effectiveness of my communication and presentation. If there was confusion, I immediately guided the team members.

Imagine ignoring my coworkers' feedback and doubling down and delivering "straightforward" scientific data. Just think if I left the meeting and created new trendlines, retitled the heading, and focused on the color of the bar graphs. I would have wasted more time and resources and failed in communication.

However, I was bothered by knowing that I wasted time, money and resources. It was a costly communication fumble. I bruised my communicator resume and made a commitment to continue growing my skill set. As I continued my career, my presentations grew in diversity and complexity. I was ready to expand my skills and focus on increasing my effectiveness in all communication formats. Seeking continual development, I strengthened and improved my listening skills. I shifted my focus to the questions from my audience. These questions were a window to their comprehension and top concerns, allowing me to communicate at a deeper level and achieve many more golden moments.

Effective communication requires "bridging and assisting" in the communication.

During a growth moment in our division, we started hiring and received an exceptional resume. On paper, this was the proper skill set for us. This person had deep science skills, succeeded wildly, and was an experienced product developer. Excited and thrilled to have this interview, we met in the lobby and quickly moved to the interview room. As we started the interview, he seemed nervous; his voice strength fluctuated, and he was stumbling on his words. I knew deep inside there was gold; it was my job to extract his greatness. So, I intentionally offered a "bridging and assisting" moment. I felt like he needed a minute to calm down. I told him I needed water and asked permission to leave the room. I came back with two bottles of water and a different interview strategy. In "bridging and assisting", I uncovered a passion and commitment that was perfect for our team. I hired him, and he was an incredible asset.

Sometimes, the interviewer fails to recognize the stress the interviewee is under and quickly deems the candidate not a fit. However, recognizing that this was a "bridging and assisting" opportunity resulted in a golden moment.

It is a lot of work to communicate effectively. Some days, communication is perfect and some days, it can be a train wreck of misunderstanding and misinterpretation.

A simple communication error might have minimal impact, can be fixed quickly, and might have little or no long-term effect. However, the large train wreck of ineffective communication can be financially impactful, cause damage to reputation, impact teams, and possibly change the long-term trajectory of a company.

Effective communication requires "pivoting" in the communication.

Many years ago, I was leading a food product division. Our team formed a partnership with a consumer products goods company, and we were in full product item development. It was a complex communication network as we operated globally, worked in different time zones, and faced language barriers. To manage and execute swift decision-making, I assisted our project manager. Occasionally, minor communication problems would arise, and "pivoting" the message was needed. The project was going well. We built our reputation and established ourselves as high-performing product developers and responsive industry experts with a keen sense of business.

The development of the product item reached completion, and we were approaching the "product ship window". This product shipped via a highly complex supply chain with delivery to Brazil. Shipping was estimated to take ten to twelve weeks and required appointments with transportation carriers, shipping docks, ports, and ocean tankers.

The day to ship the product finally arrived, and a small group of team members assembled at the shipping dock. We saw the tractor-trailer coming down the road, it turned into our parking lot, and excitement built. It was thirty months of arduous work by countless committed team members. It was happening. We were shipping!

The driver puts the truck in reverse. The safety alarm is beeping, and our excitement intensifies! He reaches the dock, stops, puts on the brake, opens the driver's door, and jumps out of the truck. He is holding the shipping manifest, and in a "straightforward" communication style, he delivers twelve powerful words: "It won't fit. You can't fit all that product in this truck."

He continues silently "measuring" our response. He can see our blank stares and confusion. He actively starts "bridging and assisting" the communication by explaining, "Refrigerator tractor trailers and ambient trailers are the same length, but refrigerator trailer capacity is 25 percent less."

We continue with blank stares, and he delivers the "pivoting" message: "It won't fit. I can't make this truck magically bigger. I am sorry."

There is silence. No one says a word, not one word! Then, one of my team members blurts out, "Oh No! we can't ship all the products? Holy cow, thirty months of hard work, and we can't ship?" In these situations, immediately following comprehension can be panic and stress. A few team members were starting to panic. One team member was pacing and rapidly reciting the extensive and complex shipping supply chain, "Warehouses, trucks, ports, and tanker reservations – *oh my gosh thirty* months of hard work."

There was no simple, fast fix! We did not budget for two shipping expenses, we only had one tanker reservation. The cork-popping champagne moment became a scramble of quick solutions, impact reduction, and reputation rebuild. The communication gap bruised the team. It took a few seconds to rally from the unfortunate news, but we decided to fill the truck and ship what we had. Locked and loaded, the truck careened down the road.

Our project manager assembled the cross-functional team, and we went into solution mode. When you only deliver a portion of the material to your customer, it can cause many production problems and have significant cost implications.

As the Director, it was my responsibility to communicate the problem. However, before I engaged our customer, I prepared.

I needed to pull my advanced communication skills together and acknowledge the impact of the problem.

During the phone call, I began relaying the situation in simple, "straightforward" communication. I actively "measuring" their response. There was silence. I moved into "bridging and assisting" and started explaining the tractor trailer size constraints. The silence continued. I was "pivoting" rapidly and said, "You are only getting 75 percent of the order, we made a mistake".

Effective communication must be "achieved".

 It was critical on this call they we "achieved" communication – a mutual understating of the situation. Once they understood they were only getting 75 percent of the order, the questions started. I had the communication skill set and ability to oscillate rapidly between *straightforward, measuring, bridging and assisting, and pivoting until we achieved - the golden moment.*

In the end, we learned that our customers were minimally impacted as they had ordered extra materials. While I would have preferred not to have had the problem, strongly developed communication skills allowed the navigation of this critical moment. Ultimately, we understood them, and they understood us in a complex high-stakes moment.

Effective communication is challenging; it takes work, commitment, and intentionality.

I hope I have inspired a moment of reflection and stirred fearless curiosity to evaluate your communication journey. Think about those communication golden moments. Think about those communication train wreck moments. Could one of these tools save time, money, or a relationship? Could one of these tools be used to achieve a golden communication moment? I encourage use of the below tools to deliver effective communication:

- **_Effective communication requires a "straightforward" exchange between a speaker and a listener._**

  Consider "straightforward" exchange as the first step in communication. A speaker speaks and the listener listens. At this stage, there is a risk that full comprehension is not achieved.

- **_Effective communication requires "measuring" the audience's comprehension_**

  Consider "measuring" as the second step and an advancing communication skill. As a speaker, you are intentionally "measuring" the effectiveness of communication. The speaker is actively looking for indicators of comprehension.

- **_Effective communication requires "bridging and assisting" in the communication._**

  Consider "bridging and assisting" as the third step of communication where the speaker is talking. The speaker recognizes the communication is not effective. The speaker intentionally helps the communication by "bridging and assisting" to ensure communication is achieved.

- **_Effective communication requires "pivoting" in the communication._**

  Consider "pivoting" to be the fourth step in communication. It is that moment in communication where the speaker is aware that there is a communication gap. They intentionally pick different words, and different ways to communicate the message.

- **_Effective communication must be "achieved"._**

  Consider "achieved" as the last step in the communication journey. It is the golden moment! The speaker has used every tool – "straightforward", "measuring", "bridging and *assisting", and "pivoting". The communication continues until the content is understood and communication is achieved.*

Every single person seeks to communicate. It does not matter if you are a student in college, a corporate executive, a fantastic truck driver, or an aspiring TedX speaker; seek gold in your communication.

I would love to help you grow and expand your communication skills. Please continue the conversation at sheila@whickedresults.com . I love to hear from my readers!

We all have the desire to communicate; it is critical to be understood and to understand others.

About the Author

Sheila Jones is a passionate communications coach. During her career, she was inspired to continually develop her skills and find ways to communicate across diverse workforces and business industries. Sheila has held leadership positions with Nestle, Campbell Soup, Walmart, and Savencia Fromage and Dairy and was responsible for leading billion-dollar business divisions.

Today, she is the CEO of Whicked Results and teaches communication skills to industry leaders and inspiring TedX speakers. Her recent industry success includes delivering an Editor's Pick for a TedX client in York Beach, Maine. She is a Maxwell Leadership Certified Team Member and Maxwell DISC Certified Behavioral Consultant. Additionally, she is a contributing author for *Emerging Leaders Magazine* and is an award-winning children's book author.

Feel free to continue the conversation via email: sheila@whickedresults.com

Into the Eye of the Hurricane and Up the Spiral of Business Growth

Brad Smith

The purpose of business is to serve customers and grow net revenue. There are capacity constraints and blocks to business growth from the first day a business is started that continue at every level beyond. Seeing and understanding those constraints, then learning and inventing your way through them, is a big part of why business growth is so slow. I want you to be able to see, understand, and move through those constraints to make your business grow as fast, effectively, efficiently, and enduringly as possible.

Most people think that production and sales are the first limiting issues of a business. They come second. The first constraint each of us has in business is our awareness and understanding of our current circumstances. Our ordinary situational awareness is never the whole truth of how things are. Every day you are alive and in business, your insights and the path forward have information gaps. Seeing, knowing, and then being able to solve these constraint problems are crucial to growth. The next step is designing and building processes that consistently resolve the specific constraint.

Reducing your current situation awareness handicap takes practice and experience. I would have you consider building a habit of listing your unanswered questions, frustrations, and what you think you need to know. Make that part of your daily and weekly review habits. (I might add, read *Atomic Habits* by James Clear.) Read your lists just before you sleep and write down the epiphanies you get when you wake up. This habit helped me solve what I considered to be impossible situations.

Awareness of your business situation and regular reviews build your ability to continuously know, see, and understand your current situation. Your job in growing a company is to understand the increasing complexity of efforts and then distill them to simplicity regularly for clarity of understanding and communication. There are six major sections to a business most professionals know as production, sales, marketing, finance, talent/culture, and, finally, research and development for product invention.

WATCH OUTCOMES

Watch the outcomes in each of the six significant sections at each new level of expansion and change. Like a beaker you fill with a new chemical and want to boil, you create the conditions for the desired results you seek and then observe the results. Awareness of outcomes, not assumptions, is how to test your theories at each stage and with each new process you build as you step up your company's evolutionary growth spiral.

How often are your theories accurate? How often are you wrong? What do your results teach you aboutyourself, your insights, accuracy, and specific habits from your previous business training, experience, and skill sets?

What do the results tell you about how you measure success, the processes you've designed, and the organization you have built so far? Watch, adjust, and always ask for team input. Our perspectives are always limited, and wisdom requires being a constant learner. That is the design of this earth. Learning is always right in front of us; awareness matters. We can learn from whispers, epiphanies, stated questions, or brick walls. Ignoring the whispers, epiphanies, and questions, we learn from running into brick walls. Which do you choose?

SALES

The common belief is that the sales process presents the product features and benefits, and then the customer will say yes and buy. The more complex sales practice is to ask questions to understand the customer's needs, wants, and pain points. The goal is to build rapport, establish trust, and offer a solution that fits the customer's desires. A subtler side of sales starts with rapport and includes values, character traits, and demonstrated reliability and honesty it takes to build trust.

If used well, the sales process provides an opportunity to use the information about the customer's needs to tailor your marketing content, generate new designs, and develop new products and services that meet and exceed customer needs and expectations.

PRODUCT DEVELOPMENT

The nuances and genius of product research and development come from the overlap of intense, thorough, and patient listening from the sales and marketing processes, insights, and good communication with the product development team. The customer wish list and customer perspectives combined with the expertise, insight, intuition, and creative evolution of the research team can generate new and innovative solutions and products or services. This is where the magic of large company's growth actually happens.

COMPANY EVOLUTION – DELEGATION

Evolutionary business growth is a spiral and starts with the entrepreneur doing everything. As the business grows, the entrepreneur can begin hiring additional staff when cash flow increases. How do you know when it is time to hire extra resources? Start with what I call the plate exercise. Write all the tasks you do in a week or month and the time they take. Then, determine which ones you should no longer be doing or are the easiest to delegate effectively to someone else. This process will help you decide when and how to evolve your business organization chart. Review this process quarterly and every time you realize you need more concentrated time to address issues only you, the owner, can tackle. That is your trigger for this habit.

If you are operating and growing a larger company, have all the managers go through the plate exercise every quarter and discuss their delegation needs and how they overlap. This discussion will increase their understanding of how the organizational chart and business needs evolve.

Scaling a company from the circumstances you are currently in, of course, starts with questions. Do you need more customers? Have you reached the stage where an increase in customers outstrips your capacity to produce products or provide services? If the answer is no, sales and marketing should be the first focus. This would be the time to review sales results, training, accountability, and management processes for the organization.

Sometimes, it may be time to replace team members, as your business may require a different type of salesperson. Here are some resources that will help you think through this challenge. Read *Secrets of Question-Based Selling* by Thomas Freese. Then, read *Cracking the Sales Management Code* by Jason Jordan. Interestingly enough, both helped me with my leadership and coaching skills.

What type of salespeople do you need? Hunters only find new customers and often aren't good at maintaining relationships. Farmer salespeople maintain and deepen customer relationships. Sometimes, a hunter can grow your business and hand it to a farmer to keep the customer relationships healthy. Do you need to figure out how to hire a hard-to-find and rare hunter? If your current sales team has rigorous and consistent processes that generate leads, build relationships, close sales, and retain customers, add salespeople to generate additional business. There are assessments, such as at Salestestonline. com, that can help you better determine your sales type needs.

EXPANSION CHALLENGES

When your new customer flow reaches where you require more production capacity, design the actions and results needed to match the increased volume. Production expansion requires building facilities, hiring staff members, and training new hires to understand the practices, values, and processes to do the right thing at the right time with full accountability.

This interwoven growth process continues up the spiral of scaling revenue expansion. Each zero you add to your top-line income will significantly change your organization and focus. Even changing your annual growth rate from 15 to 30 percent or doubling your expansion rate has the equivalent impact on how to view, plan, and design changes in your company and its processes.

HIRING

If your sales growth is dialed in, the next expansion focus is hiring talent that matches your company values, culture, and customer relationships. A simple way to think through the hiring pipeline process is to review the delegation list generated by the plate exercise process (mentioned above).

The delegation list of positions triggers the hiring process to address the expansion needs. Start with generating a list of needed results. Then, build a task or action list to produce the desired results. What are the skills required to create those results? Next, identify the character traits for each position that make the skills and results almost automatic and easily accomplished. These character traits could include honesty, work ethic, commitment, collaboration, and more.

This essential list of character traits required for hiring each position is far more critical than many suspect. For example, someone good at detail and numbers might not be a good match for a receptionist role, the first point of contact with the public. I have always separated sales and marketing because the type of person who excels at marketing is usually not good at sales generation. These are two very different types of people. Salespeople are focused on getting the sale; most are money driven and good (hopefully) at interpersonal interactions. While marketing people analyze why customers buy, what channels and methods work best to reach them, and focus on information gathering.

When hiring, consider the values and character traits that align with the culture you want to create and maintain. Every company's culture is different, even within the same industry sector. Also crucial to the culture is how that works with your customers. Over time, conscious culture creation and sustainability are hidden aspects of company growth and evolution that are frequently overlooked or ignored.

HARDEST EXERCISE

The results you want to create in your business almost always reflect you both consciously and unconsciously. I am suggesting an exercise so that you can get a handle on that first. Start by asking yourself, "Who am I? What are my character traits? Which ones support my business success, and which will hold me back?" This may be the most critical exercise I give you. Write who you are and your best and worst character traits. Then, go ask a close friend, spouse, or partner to write your worst traits and then your best and talk through them together. Design who you will be that will best allow you to succeed in your business adventure. Attention, focus, and repetition with commitment can modify any trait. Think of your character as a collection of habits you chose before you were verbal and now choose to consciously, proactively, alter by design.

FINANCIALS

I ask every CEO client I coach to maintain at least five numbers in their head: cash in the bank, invoices and collections due this month, expenses for the month, net profit for the month, and new sales that will close at month's end. This practice ensures they know where they are constantly at a macro level, have a good understanding of and information flow from the financial team, and can make spending decisions as required. This constant review by the CEO keeps the financial team honest, accurate, and accountable. It also requires good communication with the sales team regarding effectiveness.

The evolution of the financial team goes from bookkeepers to hiring an accounting manager. As the business grows, the services of a controller are required. The CEO should be reviewing the financials, not generating them. A suitable controller can manage analysis and reporting until the financial overview requires a more in-depth understanding of the strategic plan and how to create the information necessary for the CEO to be fully informed about business results. As business revenue grows, the services of a part-time CFO will eventually be required. This evolution continues until the financial overview is a big enough time cost to have a full-time CFO on staff.

PRODUCTION

Scaling the production process is pretty straightforward, most of the time. If your production process is done one piece at a time, then the pricing is appropriately high. If your production is done in batches, you can add more chunks with specific weekly output rates. Sometimes, batching scaleup can be engineered into a continuous process that can run intermittently. The next leap is a continuous operation 24/7, with appropriate increases always in storage and shipping facilities capacity.

All evolutionary stages, from single to continuous, require a learning curve with many challenges to learn your way through. All the stages require sales volume to match output. They also require cost-benefit analysis and hiring and training additional staff to monitor and run the processes. Giving up profit to move to continuous production in the short term is OK, but never in the long term. Always with production scaling, volume and capacity are tuned appropriately, and profits are watched and managed at the design level first. I have done every version of production scaling. Each one had its frustrations and was challenging, intriguing, and, from the proper perspective, fun. This takes motivation, objectivity, and commitment to achieve.

COORDINATED CHANGE ENVISIONING

Business growth requires scaling every aspect of the business in a coordinated manner, much like the choreography of a dance troupe. Your ability to envision all the moving parts' impacts simultaneously must keep growing to move consciously from the current situation through learning to the future designed state of continuous growth. Business growth is not a short-term project. It requires commitment, determination, patience, and persistence. Business growth is a marathon.

MOTIVATION

Knowing and growing your reason for even being in business is critical to the energy for achievement behind the growth. *Why* do you want to wake up each day, go to work, and grow your business? If your answer is money only, I always say garbage.

Money is a tool. Money allows you to feel financially safe, capable, and productive. Money even supports self-worth. It allows you to afford the life you want, care for people you love, buy a house or three, go on vacations, build a retirement, or even impact the world. My why evolved when I realized how much energy I got from the insights I led my clients to, which opened up new vistas and triggered their epiphanies. I got a boost when I knew the string of insights and epiphanies they would have to go through when they were ready and finally got them an additional zero in their top-line revenue and net profit. Your motivation and enthusiasm will change as your company grows. Self-inspiration is the key to your leadership and inspiring your employees to be their best and most fun.

GROWTH INTERACTION

Every time you change a process in one business section, every other section will be impacted and may need to be adjusted. Small and medium-sized companies drive revenue growth with sales supported by every other part: production, marketing, talent acquisition and training, finance, and product development. At the top end of business size, research and product development drive growth, which then flows to the other five sections. The interaction is continuous.

I measure the effectiveness of companies by asking a few questions. What is your gross revenue annually? What is the total headcount in the business? Then, I divide revenue by employee count, giving me the $/employee measure. You can use the same measure for countries or states, $ GDP/citizen. It is also essential to look at the industry average $/employee while you are at it. Then, I ask what the revenue and employee count year-over-year growth was over the last five years. This allows me to look at the culture, operations, hiring, sales and marketing, and training process effectiveness and quality. This is a macro-measurement for company effectiveness. It also exposes management's ability to view, adjust, and evolve the company. I have yet to find a company below the largest multibillion-dollar size that can't build growth to 100 percent a year. How would you improve your growth rate to 100 percent a year?

The most substantial limitation to growth is almost always the management's ability to hold all the moving parts and their outcomes interactively in their mind's future vision. One purpose of executive teams is to segment the growth management load to the company's different functions and have them mentally carry the change impact details. It reduces the mental load and increases the requirement for frequent, thorough, deep communication.

The depth and thoroughness of communication need simplicity and accuracy. Building focus, alignment, enthusiasm, energy, and active pursuit of specific tactical actions grows companies significantly.

Finally, realize that each zero or even half zero of revenue growth requires coordinated process changes in all six business sections. From startups to multibillion-dollar companies, each growth level is evolving you first, then the business. Be proactive in the growth by design rather than reactive and knee-jerk. Plan, design, think, and review. The reason we feel accomplished when we grow a company is putting so much of ourselves, way more than you can imagine, in the evolutionary spiral.

Books suggested: *Atomic Habits* by James Clear, *Secrets of Question-Based Selling* by Thomas Freese, and *Cracking the Sales Management Code* by Jason Jordan.

ABOUT THE AUTHOR

Brad Smith is the founder and CEO of Stellar Insight Inc., a business growth consulting and coaching company. Brad has been a chemist, production plant and equipment designer, business manager, business consultant, and executive coach for CEOs and business owners. He constantly pursues insight into business success, organizational excellence, and the practical actions it takes to achieve significant business growth consistently. In his words, "Everything is a theory until you experience it and can consciously repeat the experiment." He coaches CEOs, business owners, and legislators for organizational growth and excellence. He has worked extensively with various industries for more than 25 years. Those companies who fully commit to the work almost always achieve significant results.

He limits his work to ambitious, curious CEOs, business owners, and teams committed to their company's excellence and growth. He also runs a Master Class for deep intuition development for CEOs and R&D teams.

Education:

1987 BS: Oregon State University, Business Management, minor in Chemistry & Psychology
1991 MBA: University Of Oregon, Marketing
Graduate of Coach University
Stellar Insight Inc. (360) 260-0138 www.stellarinsightinc.com
brad.smith@stellarinsightinc.com, Vancouver, WA

CRAFTING YOUR GENIUS BRAND

SHELBY JO LONG

THE GENIUS FACTOR

When you align your brand with your unique skills, talents, or genius, you're not just another service provider or product creator. You become a singular entity in a sea of sameness. Your genius could be an unparalleled skill, a unique perspective, or even a new approach to solving a timeless problem. It sets you apart in a meaningful way, allowing your business to compete and dominate in your niche.

Brands that succeed are the ones that form emotional connections with their audience. It's not just about having the best product or the most efficient service; it's about resonating on a level that logic can't reach. When people feel an emotional pull, they're more likely to engage, recommend, and remain loyal to your brand. By branding around your genius, you allow for an emotional story that naturally draws people in, aligns with their needs or values, and keeps them coming back.

When you create a brand around your genius, the message you put out into the world isn't just another sales pitch; it's a narrative that people can relate to. Perhaps it's the story of how you discovered your genius or how your unique skills have solved a problem many have struggled with. This narrative is a harmonizing force that makes your brand's message resonate with those who come across it. Once that resonance is established, converting a casual browser into a committed customer is far easier.

In the digital world, authenticity is currency. People are tired of polished corporate-speak and insincerity. They crave real connections and seek out those whom they feel are genuine. When your brand is an authentic reflection of your genius— your true self—it speaks to the audience in a way that most other brands cannot.

What starts as a connection with a single customer or client can quickly ripple outward. Word of mouth, especially in the digital sphere, is incredibly potent. A single positive review or testimonial can be amplified exponentially, attracting more people to your brand. The emotional connection strengthens this ripple effect, as people are likelier to share experiences that have touched them emotionally.

Your brand story is not merely a recounting of your business history; it's an emotional journey you share with your audience. It integrates your unique genius—an innovative product, unparalleled service, or unique business model—into a compelling narrative. The more you can make that narrative resonate emotionally, the more memorable and impactful your brand will be. When people feel a personal connection to your story, they're far more likely to invest in your products or services.

By incorporating your genius into your brand's narrative, you position yourself as more than just a vendor; you become a guide or coach in your clients' journey toward transformation. Whether offering business consulting, health solutions, or tech innovation, your unique skills help solve specific problems or fulfill particular needs. You offer solutions and pathways for transformation—educating, inspiring, and actively guiding your clients toward better versions of themselves or their businesses. This personalized, transformational experience elevates your brand, making it not just a choice but a trusted resource.

Once a transaction is complete, the traditional business-client relationship often ends. But when you've positioned yourself as a guide and mentor, the relationship doesn't just continue; it deepens. Clients become advocates, fans, and even community members centered around your brand and its genius. They are more likely to return for additional services and to recommend you to their networks. As this community grows, it provides a fertile ground for continued business and further serves to authenticate your brand's promise of transformation.

Genius is not an isolated quality; it thrives best in a supportive, interactive environment. When you build a community around your genius idea, you're not just strengthening your brand but enhancing your capabilities and discovering new directions for your genius to evolve. Feedback, insights, and testimonials from your clients offer real-time data you can use to refine and adapt your offerings. As your clients transform, so do you in response to their needs and successes. The community becomes a collaborative think-tank where your genius is continually tested, adapted, and reinvigorated.

The deepened relationship with your client base and the community around your genius creates an invaluable feedback loop. You can adapt quicker to market needs, fine-tune your services, and develop new offerings, directly catering to your audience's requirements. Therefore, your genius doesn't exist in a bubble but is continually evolving, spurred by the transformations you affect in your clients.

Integrating your genius into your brand story and client relationships creates a virtuous cycle. Your brand's emotional resonance attracts and retains clients; your role as a guide facilitates their transformations, deepens relationships, and builds a community; and the continual interaction and feedback within this community refine and amplify your genius. This synergistic relationship is the keystone of a robust, resilient, and ever-evolving brand.

Assigning a monetary value to your genius is a delicate but necessary step. This phase goes beyond just pricing a product or service; it's about quantifying the transformative potential you offer. It's an assertion that your unique skills, experiences, and solutions have concrete worth. However, this can be a double-edged sword. Price too low, and you risk devaluing your genius, turning it into a commodity. If the price is too high without adequate justification, the marketplace will likely reject it.

Once you've assigned a value to your genius, the next step is entering the marketplace—a landscape flooded with businesses vying for consumer attention, especially in the digital world. This is where many genius entrepreneurs find themselves at a crossroads. You're not merely selling a service or product; you're selling a unique solution that embodies your specialized skill set. This changes how you attract your ideal clients, setting up a more complex but potentially rewarding sales funnel.

In a crowded digital marketplace, general advertising often amounts to shouting into the void. Success comes from precision—knowing who your ideal clients are, their problems, and how your genius can solve them. You'll need to employ more sophisticated marketing strategies, from SEO to social media advertising, to analytics and possibly even machine learning algorithms that can identify and target individuals most likely to be receptive to your offering.

The marketplace doesn't lack options; it lacks clarity. A well-articulated brand story serves as your North Star in an environment of choices. This narrative should weave together who you are, what you offer, and, most importantly, why it matters. But it's not enough to tell your story; you must show tangible proof of your genius at work—results, transformations, success stories, testimonials, etc.

If your genius does indeed have transformative potential, then highlighting real-world examples of this transformation becomes your ultimate selling point. Showcase your success stories and, if possible, let your satisfied clients become your brand's ambassadors. When potential clients can see the tangible benefits that others have gained from your services, it becomes much easier to envision how they would similarly benefit. This creates a compelling case for why your genius solution is not just different but better—more effective, reliable, or comprehensive than the competition offers.

In a digital world awash with information, standing out requires a blend of art and science. The art is crafting a compelling brand story that resonates deeply with your ideal clients. The science is leveraging various digital marketing tools to ensure this story reaches those clients efficiently and cost-effectively. When these elements are combined, your brand becomes more than just another option in a crowded marketplace; it becomes the go-to solution for a specific problem, for a particular group of people, and in a unique way that only your genius can provide.

Your brand story isn't just a surface-level marketing gimmick; it's the comprehensive narrative that encapsulates your core values, vision, and, most importantly, your unique genius process. It's a living document that evolves as you grow, but its central theme remains consistent: who you are and the value you bring. Crafting a compelling brand story is not just about self-expression; it's about framing your journey and expertise in a way that resonates emotionally with your target audience.

ROLE OF THE GENIUS PROCESS IN YOUR BRAND STORY

The genius process is essentially the secret sauce of your brand. It's the unique methodology or system you've developed that solves a specific problem in an innovative way. This is what differentiates you from competitors. When you infuse this genius process into your brand story, you're giving your audience a tour behind the curtain, allowing them to see what makes your solution stand out. More importantly, you're letting them witness the transformative power of your services, which helps elevate your offering from a mere transaction to an emotional experience.

While the tale of your journey and the description of your genius process are integral for emotional resonance, they also serve a practical function: establishing your credibility. Testimonials, case studies, industry recognition, and educational background can all contribute to bolstering your credibility. But credibility isn't just established through accolades; it's also built by consistently delivering on your promises. This is why it's crucial to show, and not just tell, the results that clients can expect.

People are naturally skeptical and have become even more so in the digital age, filled with dubious claims and fake testimonials. Therefore, when potential clients consider investing in a transformative process, they have several key questions: What exactly will they get out of it? How long will it take? What is required of them? Your brand story should proactively address these concerns, ideally through relatable examples and compelling visuals that allow them to see the journey they're about to embark upon.

It's not enough to promise a transformation; you have to prove it. This often means providing measurable outcomes beyond anecdotal evidence in today's data-driven landscape. Whether it's a percentage increase in productivity, a significant uptick in customer satisfaction, or a quantifiable improvement in quality of life, these hard numbers offer prospective clients a tangible understanding of what they can expect in return for their investment.

When clients invest in a transformation—especially with a more premium price tag—they aren't just buying a service and a new reality. They must understand what to anticipate throughout the process and how their lives or businesses will change. This means your brand story needs to speak to the before and after authentically and believably. Authenticity is critical; overselling or under-delivering can damage your brand's credibility.

GENIUS ENTREPRENEURSHIP: THE UNFOLDING OF EXPERTISE INTO ENTERPRISE

Genius entrepreneurship isn't about starting a business for the sake of business alone; it's about transforming your unique expertise —your genius—into a viable, impactful business model. This requires a kind of entrepreneurial alchemy where your deep skills and insights are converted into services or products that fulfill a specific market need. The cornerstone of this transformation is clarity—clarity in your niche, the problems you solve, and the impact of your solution.

Operating within a clearly defined niche does several things for you as a genius entrepreneur. First, it ensures you are playing to your strengths. You're not trying to be everything to everyone; you are focusing on being extraordinary in a particular domain. This directly affects the quality of service you provide and your reputation in the market.

A clear niche also allows for a higher quality of interaction with clients. When you specialize, you attract more ideal clients and understand their problems granularly. This depth of understanding fosters trust, makes for more meaningful service delivery, and leads to solid repeat business. A specialized service or product that naturally delivers on its promise encourages a healthy referral flow, often the lifeblood of small, expert-led businesses.

When you operate in a niche, you can more easily spot trends, identify gaps, and predict future needs within your specific sector. This puts you in a fantastic position to innovate. You're not just pushing out generic products or services but developing targeted solutions that can make a real impact. And because you've built a community of trusting clients, you have a built-in test audience for these new solutions. Innovation becomes a participatory process, deepening your clients' investment in your brand and enabling you to refine offerings before a broader release.

Serving a niche audience also means you can hone your marketing and communication skills specifically for that group. The language, the pain points, the aspirations—understanding these elements for a specific audience allows for highly targeted and resonant communication. This isn't just about speaking their language; it's about delivering messages that can penetrate the noise and distractions that typically inundate consumers. This level of resonance builds trust, which is the foundation for any long-term business relationship.

Once trust is established, it becomes a platform for expansion—but not necessarily into different niches or industries. Sometimes, the most potent form of growth is deeper into the community you already serve. As you solve more complex problems or introduce more innovative solutions, you solidify your status as an expert and leader. This expands your business and deepens your impact within your chosen community, thus fulfilling the essence of genius entrepreneurship.

In an increasingly complex and competitive business landscape, professionals who can offer multilayered solutions to their clients hold a distinct advantage. They don't just deliver a service; they become an integral part of their client's journey. This leads to deeper trust, stronger relationships, and, often, lifelong clients. Let's explore how different professionals embody this ideal in their unique sectors.

Consider an accountant who isn't just punching numbers or filling out tax forms. This accountant acts as a financial sherpa, guiding small businesses through the treacherous terrains of fiscal responsibility, regulatory compliance, and strategic planning. They adapt to the ever-changing needs of their clients, growing from a mere service provider to an indispensable business advisor. The accountant might introduce more advanced services like asset management, investment planning, or succession planning as the business scales. By offering such a comprehensive suite of services, they insert themselves into multiple critical aspects of the business lifecycle, fortifying their indispensability.

Similarly, a chiropractor who offers more than just spinal adjustments but provides a holistic health program has a far more significant impact on their clients' lives. Immediate pain relief might be the entry point, but nutrition advice, a tailored fitness program, and ongoing wellness check-ins keep clients engaged in the long term. This type of chiropractor understands that health is a continuous journey and offers solutions that clients might not even have realized they needed. The result is a loyal clientele who sees the chiropractor as a partner in their overall well-being, not just a quick fix for acute issues.

A marketing agency that can take a business from brand conceptualization to market dominance becomes invaluable. They are not just about making flashy ads but about understanding a brand's essence, competitive landscape, and growth trajectory. This agency will have tools for data analytics, consumer insights, digital advertising, and long-term strategy, thus offering a one-stop solution for all marketing needs. Clients rely on this agency as an external extension of their internal team, knowing they have a trusted partner who understands where they are and, more importantly, where they need to go.

These examples are adaptable and eager to evolve to meet their clients' growing and changing needs. By consistently solving multiple, sometimes unarticulated, problems for their clients, they deepen the level of trust and connection, making it less likely for clients to look elsewhere for additional services.

It's not just about offering multiple services; it's about integrating them to make the client's life or business run more smoothly. When services are integrated, the value provided is not just additive; it's exponential. Clients begin to see these professionals not just as vendors but as essential partners in their journey—whether toward better financial health, physical well-being, or market success.

The first step for any professional aiming to be indispensable is identifying a precise audience whose problems they can solve exceptionally well. By profoundly understanding who they serve, these professionals are better positioned to tailor their solutions, making them more relevant, impactful, and, ultimately, sought-after. This isn't merely about identifying a market gap; it's about aligning one's skills, tools, and resources to create bespoke solutions that provide actual value.

Beyond solving immediate issues, these professionals understand the significance of nurturing long-term client relationships. It's a foresight that makes them more than just service providers; it elevates them into trusted advisors. A long-term investment isn't about customer retention alone; it's a commitment to the client's evolving needs, anticipating future problems, and being prepared with solutions or advice when the time comes.

Take, for instance, a real estate agent who embodies this principle excellently. The role of a real estate agent could easily be transactional—find a house, sell a house, and move on. However, agents who recognize the emotional, financial, and logistical complexities involved in buying or selling a home transform themselves into journey navigators for their clients.

From the moment you decide to sell your current home, this agent is with you, advising on market timing home-staging tips and even bringing in or recommending contractors for quick fixes to enhance your home's market value. They don't just stop at helping you sell; they also assist in identifying your next dream home.

But it goes beyond that. They help you choose neighborhoods that align with your lifestyle and needs—be it proximity to good schools, ease of commute, or local amenities. They provide or connect you with financial advisors to help you understand mortgage options, property taxes, and other fiscal aspects of your purchase.

Life rarely goes exactly as planned. Perhaps your home takes longer to sell than anticipated, or maybe the inspection of your new dream home reveals some unexpected issues. A genuinely indispensable real estate agent foresees these bumps and helps you navigate them. They negotiate contingencies, offer alternatives, and sometimes even liaise with contractors to expedite essential repairs. They make a potentially stressful process not just bearable but as smooth and hassle-free as possible.

By assuming a comprehensive role in your journey of changing homes, they earn your trust and pave the way for future collaborations and referrals. You won't think twice about recommending this agent to friends or family or writing a glowing review. Why? Because they have moved beyond being a mere service provider and become a pivotal part of a significant chapter in your life.

In sum, professionals who master the art of identifying their audience, crafting precise solutions, and investing in long-term relationships stand out as invaluable assets in their clients' lives. They elevate their service from a mere transaction to an enriching experience, transforming clients into lifelong advocates for their expertise.

The genius of an entrepreneur or a business leader doesn't just lie in their expertise or the initial innovation they bring to the market. It resides in how adaptable they are to the needs and challenges of their evolving audience. Your genius becomes a living, dynamic entity when you tune it to the market's pulse, allowing you to create an inclusive community around your ideas.

This community isn't just a set of consumers; it's a collaborative ecosystem where your clients become advocates, beta testers, and even contributors to your thought leadership. Your solutions evolve based on honest feedback and actual needs, giving your brand an organic vitality that canned solutions can't replicate.

Every entrepreneurial journey comes with its ebbs and flows. Economic conditions fluctuate, consumer behaviors mutate, and even the most well-oiled production systems can hit snags. Mental resilience is your compass through these inevitable challenges. Preparation doesn't just mean having a business continuity plan; it means developing the emotional intelligence to keep your head on straight when things are unplanned.

Let's be candid: Not every idea you have will resonate with the market. There might be periods of low engagement and, at times, outright rejection of what you thought was a revolutionary concept. This isn't just a business challenge; it's a test of your resilience and adaptability.

Your genius comes into play here as you pivot your approach. Perhaps the market isn't ready for your solution, or your communication style needs an overhaul to simplify the complex. Being able to pivot is not a sign of failure but an indicator of your versatility and understanding of market dynamics.

The resilience of your genius comes from a meticulously crafted plan. It starts with a strategic outline that defines your goals, the problems you're solving, and the methodologies you'll employ. This plan serves as a framework that's robust enough to guide you but flexible enough to adapt to the ever-changing business landscape.

The success of your genius also hinges on how well you communicate it. Adjusting your communication style to suit your audience's changing preferences or diversifying your channels to reach a broader demographic can make all the difference. Your ability to articulate your value can significantly influence how your genius is received and how much impact it can generate.

THE ART OF SKILLFUL LEVERAGE IN BUSINESS AND ENTREPRENEURSHIP

In the competitive landscape of business and entrepreneurship, the ability to leverage—be it skills, resources, or relationships—can serve as your unique advantage. Leveraging is not merely utilizing what you have; it is the strategic amplification of your resources for optimum outcomes. Here's a deeper dive into how to leverage various aspects of your business effectively.

An in-depth grasp of your strengths and opportunities in the marketplace is the first step toward effective leverage. It requires constant market research and a data-driven understanding of where you excel. Knowing your unique selling proposition (USP) and the gaps you can fill in the market will guide you in crafting targeted strategies and positioning your services or products for maximum impact.

Your team is not just a group of employees but an extension of your capabilities. You may be exceptionally skilled in some areas, but it's unlikely that you are an expert in all facets of your business. Building a solid team allows you to fill in your competency gaps. They execute the vision and enhance your creative skills, allowing you the mental and emotional space to operate at your peak potential.

In business, you don't operate in a vacuum; relationships are crucial. Whether it's a mentor who provides invaluable advice, industry contacts who offer partnerships, or a community that provides support and resources, relationships can propel you to the next level. It's not just about networking but cultivating and sustaining relationships that offer mutual benefits.

Business is often seen as a competitive endeavor, but collaboration is equally vital. By partnering with others, you can combine resources for a more significant impact. Additionally, mentors and professional communities offer an expanded network and a wealth of experience to guide you through business challenges. They can provide a new perspective, validate your ideas, and offer insights you might not have considered.

You are most creative and innovative when operating within your genius zone. This is a mental and emotional state where your talents and passions intersect, allowing you to tackle problems and develop solutions from a place of deep insight and excitement. Here, you are not just competent but also profoundly fulfilled, which fuels your resilience and drive.

Being in a space where your talents and passions intersect is like hitting a business sweet spot. Here, you leverage your skills and draw energy from what fulfills you. This state does more than make work enjoyable; it gives you the resilience to overcome obstacles and the inspiration to innovate. You're not just working to solve problems; you're working to create a legacy.

The Power of Levity in Business: A Catalyst for Success and Innovation

Levity is often an underrated element in business. The term, generally associated with lightness and humor, extends far beyond its surface meaning when applied to a business environment. The presence of levity in your organization can become the glue that binds your team, fuels creativity, and enhances your overall business atmosphere. Here's a comprehensive look at why levity is vital and how it contributes to various aspects of business success.

A leader who naturally fosters levity creates a less stressful environment. Reduced stress levels result in a more focused and productive team. When employees feel at ease, it helps their mental well-being, translating to higher energy levels aimed at creative problem-solving and innovation.

Your ability to maintain a lighter atmosphere while being competent at what you do makes you attractive to current and prospective team members. People are more inclined to work for and with someone they genuinely enjoy being around. Your team isn't just joining for a paycheck; they're joining to be part of an environment that uplifts them.

When an organization encourages levity, the mental barriers that often hamper creativity dissolve. A relaxed atmosphere allows people to think outside the box, take calculated risks, and develop innovative solutions. Team members feel encouraged to share their wildest ideas without fearing ridicule, knowing that even an unconventional idea could be the next big thing.

Levity creates a conducive atmosphere for open dialogue. Communication isn't just about transferring information; it's about building understanding. A relaxed setting fosters a sense of trust, making team members more open to sharing their ideas, giving honest feedback, and contributing to group discussions, all of which are critical for business growth.

Shared laughter and light moments act as social glue, strengthening the bonds between team members. A tightly knit team collaborates more efficiently, which is vital for problem-solving. Strong bonds can also increase employee retention, as team members become more invested in the team's and organization's success.

A levity-rich atmosphere naturally increases the level of teamwork. When team members enjoy working together, they are more likely to pool their collective intelligence for problem-solving. The team becomes more significant than the sum of its parts, tackling challenges from various angles and finding practical solutions more rapidly.

While professionalism is crucial, it doesn't have to be stiff or stodgy. Levity allows you to strike a balance where team members maintain their professional duties while being able to express their personalities. This balance fosters a more holistic work environment where team members feel seen and valued as complete individuals.

In an atmosphere of levity, ideas are not static but dynamic. They evolve through discussions, iterations, and even jokes. This dynamic nature ensures that you're not stuck with an idea's first version but allow it to grow and mature through collective contributions.

Business landscapes are perpetually shifting, and so are the individuals who make up your team. A levity-induced atmosphere is more adaptable to these changes. The agility that comes with such an environment can help you swiftly pivot strategies or adapt to new market trends, keeping you ahead of the competition.

Creating a Lasting Legacy: The Synergy of Passion, Strengths, and Thought Leadership

When leaving a mark in the world, especially within your industry, legacy is the indelible imprint that speaks volumes about your life's work. It transcends the temporary and sets you on a course for long-lasting impact. Legacy isn't something that happens overnight; it is built step-by-step, aligning your passions, strengths, and intellectual contributions. Below, we explore various facets of creating a legacy with depth and breadth.

Your unique combination of passion and strengths is a fertile ground for thought leadership. Utilizing these traits helps you stand out in your field, offering viewpoints and solutions others may not have considered. As a thought leader, you set the pace, introduce new concepts, and challenge existing paradigms. This is a journey toward becoming an authority, a go-to person within your sector.

A key component of legacy creation is contributing to your industry's growth and knowledge base. Whether through scholarly articles, speaking engagements, or mentorship programs, your insights can help elevate the industry. When you offer invaluable expertise, you build your legacy and uplift everyone who follows in your footsteps.

As an influencer in your field, you can shape narratives around crucial topics. You can be the voice that addresses gaps, corrects misinformation, or shines a light on under-explored areas. Doing so builds your credibility and brings nuanced discussions to the forefront, thereby enriching the industry.

Turning your genius idea into tangible assets can prove your contributions. Whether you're developing patented technologies, launching digital platforms, or creating award-winning designs, these assets are milestones in your legacy journey. They give you leverage and serve as an extension of your thought leadership.

Books, digital programs, and magazines are products and tools for building authority. When your name is associated with high-quality content that helps people, your status within the marketplace naturally elevates. These tools serve as lasting records of your expertise, keeping your voice alive even when you're not in the room.

Unlike trends that come and go, a well-crafted idea has a long shelf life. When your contributions are based on deep insight and thorough research, they will likely stand the test of time. They become integral to your legacy, signifying that your work is not just a flash in the pan but a lasting contribution to the field.

A strong legacy is the sum of consistent actions aligned with your values and vision. The power of consistency lies in its ability to build trust, while values serve as the moral compass guiding those actions. An articulated vision is the roadmap, pointing toward a more significant impact.

Ultimately, the most memorable legacies leave a positive imprint within your industry and the lives of the people your work touches. Whether you're solving a significant industry problem, advancing the field with your innovations, or mentoring the next generation of leaders, the positive effects ripple far beyond your immediate circle.

CONCLUSION

The entrepreneurial journey is akin to crafting a masterpiece, weaving together various elements that reflect your genius. The composition includes leveraging your skills, creating a conducive environment for levity, and constructing a meaningful legacy. Each section of this chapter is a movement in that symphony, a fundamental part of the composition.

Starting with defining and honing your genius, we saw how crucial it is to remain attuned to your niche, serve your audience passionately, and adapt to market changes. The leverage movement highlighted the importance of capitalizing on your strengths, filling gaps with a strong team, and fostering relationships that propel you to the next level. Levity underscored the positive culture that emerges when you allow creativity and innovation to flourish, enhancing team dynamics and problem-solving capabilities. Finally, the legacy movement crystallized the long-term vision, building your brand into an enduring institution that outlasts trends and market fluctuations.

Genius, leverage, levity, and legacy are not isolated elements; they interact in a dynamic equilibrium. Your genius attracts and sustains an audience. Leverage amplifies your impact. Levity fosters a thriving work environment, and legacy is the indelible mark left by the harmonious blend of all these factors.

By internalizing the insights and strategies discussed in this chapter, you are not just walking down the entrepreneurial path but composing a symphony of success, each note resonating with the next. As you continue to navigate the complex landscapes of entrepreneurship, may this chapter serve as a compass, guiding you in realizing your fullest potential and creating a deeply fulfilling and far-reaching legacy.

ABOUT THE AUTHOR

Shelby is a highly experienced executive and global managing partner at the Strategic Advisor Board. She specializes in client management and is an expert in branding and positioning. Shelby works with some of the most influential brands in the world, helping create a strong framework for small to mid-market organizations.

A professional speaker, international speaking coach, and four-time international best-selling author, Shelby is a recognized expert in corporate communications. She works with prominent CEOs, professional athletes, and influencers in executive coaching and consulting to help companies amplify their influence in the marketplace with a comprehensive brand presence. In all her endeavors, she helps clients develop a comprehensive brand strategy for thought leadership.

Bowman Digital Media
Ira Bowman
SEO Specialist

951-902-9550

ira@bowmandigitalmedia.com

What We Do:

increase sales by generating more website traffic

How We Help:

SEO:
Search Engine Optimization includes content creation, backlink building, meta data, keyword and traffic monitoring

Website Development and Maintenance:
We are WordPress Developers

Graphic Design:
For Print or Online - Logos, Business Cards, Brochures, Custom Design Work

Photography:
Headshots, Event, Product and Lifestyle

Videography:
Video Shooting Editing

Social Media Marketing:
All Platforms Including: LinedIn, Facebook, Instagram, YouTube, Pinterest, Twitter and More.

Sales Growth by Design

www.bowmandigitalmedia.com

PROSHARK
DIGITAL SOLUTIONS

INNOVATIVE SOLUTIONS DESIGNED TO INSPIRE

What We Do:

Website Development

DIY Website Platform

Mobile App & Software Development

AdNetwork

Email Marketing

...and so much more!

Learn More

🌐 www.proshark.com

✉ info@proshark.com